# The AI Cascade Effect

By Peter Johnson

*AI Convergence in Critical Infrastructure, Healthcare, and Financial Services*

First Edition: May 2026
ISBN: 979-8-9951870-3-5
Cover Design: Mike Huddleston
Book Design: Peter Johnson
Published by: Peter Johnson
Printed in the United States

**Disclaimer**

This book provides general information and analysis regarding AI security, governance, and related topics. It does not constitute legal, financial, technical, or professional advice. Readers should consult qualified professionals before making decisions based on concepts discussed herein. The author and publisher make no warranties regarding accuracy, completeness, or applicability to any specific situation, and disclaim liability for any losses arising from reliance on this material. The threat landscape, regulations, and technologies described reflect conditions known at the time of writing and may have changed.

**A Note on Examples**

Certain organizational examples in this book are composites, hypotheticals, or fictionalized accounts informed by publicly reported incidents and established risk patterns. Where real companies, events, or individuals are discussed by name, descriptions are based on publicly available sources cited in the references. No unnamed example is intended to represent any specific organization, and any resemblance to actual institutions not explicitly identified is coincidental.

# Preface: Societal Fragility

Somewhere right now, a hospital's surgical schedule depends on an AI system it doesn't control.

That system's predictions depend on the regional power grid. The grid's AI load balancer is adjusting for an approaching storm from demand forecasts that include the hospital's own consumption patterns. Neither institution fully understands the vendor-supplied models connecting them.

When one falters, the other follows. The consequences don't stay technical; they become human.

This is not a hypothetical, it is inevitable. The only question is: which Tuesday is it?

*The AI Convergence Trap* mapped the territory. It described how AI convergence, which unifies organizational knowledge into a single intelligent layer, creates amazing efficiency and fragility as features of the same system, at the same time. It traced the dissolution of boundaries, the transformation of information from locations to gradients, the erosion of human redundancy, the governance frameworks built for a world that no longer exists.

It asked whether we would build AI convergence wisely or join the long line of organizations and vendors that optimized for efficiency, ignored the fragility efficiency creates, and discovered the cost only when it was too late. What emerged was the AI Security-Commercial Complex, an ecosystem of vendors, consultants, and platform providers whose business models depend on the persistence of the problems they claim to solve. Like the compliance industry that grew around database-era regulation, this complex is, literally, complex: a web of dependencies and incentives masquerading as progress.

So what happens when we don't?

David Habib's *"Latent Vector"*, the book that first made the economic case for enterprise AI convergence, presented the promise: an AI nervous system watching everything across your business systems, understanding it in real time, coordinating the best next actions so the organization operates as one. The economic benefits are substantial. The transformation, as Habib argues, is difficult to resist on every level.

*"The lack of humility before nature that's being displayed here staggers me."*

Does it sound familiar?

Dr. Ian Malcolm's indictment of Jurassic Park's architects applies with uncomfortable precision. They believed they had engineered control. The dinosaurs bred anyway. The fences failed anyway. Control was never more than a story they told themselves.

We are telling ourselves the same story now, at infrastructure scale.

*The AI Convergence Trap* held these visions in tension: the promise and the peril, the capability and the vulnerability, the same feature viewed from different angles.

Here we will break that tension open across the sectors where it matters most. Not all enterprises face AI convergence equally.

The retailer whose AI recommendation engine hallucinates faces embarrassment. The hospital whose diagnostic AI hallucinates faces malpractice. The utility whose grid optimization AI hallucinates faces blackouts. The bank whose trading AI fails faces cascades that propagate through interconnected markets before anyone recognizes a problem exists.

Critical infrastructure, healthcare, and financial services represent distinct configurations of the same underlying problem: what happens when organizations that society cannot afford to have fail adopt technology that creates efficiency and fragility as features of the same system?

These are not arbitrary selections. They are the sectors that nation-state adversaries and sophisticated criminal organizations already target most persistently: for strategic leverage, for ransom, for intelligence, for profit. AI convergence does not create their interest; it concentrates the value of what they're already pursuing.

The same prompt injection, three different wounds. The same hallucinations, three different body counts. The same dissolved boundary, three different catastrophes.

And when the sectors connect, when the grid failure darkens the hospital, when the hospital's billing failure cascades to the insurer, when the insurer's liquidity crisis triggers the trading algorithm, the cascade crosses every boundary we drew on organizational charts and regulatory frameworks. The dominoes are already in motion, and all that follows is where they fall.

*The AI Convergence Trap* identified the mechanisms; here they become consequences.

These dissolved boundaries appear differently in each sector. In critical infrastructure, they connect operational technology to information technology in ways legacy protocols never contemplated. In healthcare, they enable inference attacks that reconstruct what patients chose to hide. In financial services, they allow correlation across products that exposes protected information and triggers compliance violations across twelve jurisdictions simultaneously. The walls served different purposes. The absence of walls creates different disasters.

When information shifts from being stored in categories to being mapped as mathematical coordinates, it changes the geometry of exposure, creating new, sector-specific attack surfaces. A grid operator's query about maintenance scheduling drifts toward emergency shutdown procedures. A physician's question about common symptoms reveals protected diagnoses. A competitor's probe reconstructs proprietary trading strategies by navigating semantic neighborhoods. The mathematics are identical. The bleeding is local.

Prompt injection, indirect prompt injection, instruction hijacking: these aren't chatbot tricks. They exploit any system that mixes untrusted input with privileged actions. The same exploit corrupts load-balancing recommendations at the utility, poisons diagnostic suggestions at the hospital, and infiltrates fraud detection at the bank. Same vulnerability. Three wounds.

Error propagation under automation bias multiplies differently by sector. The hallucinated maintenance schedule creates equipment failures. The hallucinated diagnosis creates unnecessary surgery. The hallucinated risk assessment creates exposure that compounds until someone audits the positions. The AI doesn't know it's wrong. The humans have eleven minutes, or eleven milliseconds, to catch what the AI missed.

The timestamps in this book reflect these different speeds. Healthcare unfolds in minutes and hours; financial services cascades in milliseconds. The notation is not inconsistent. It is the argument.

Vendor opacity and model supply chains create dependencies no single institution controls. The model trained on data you cannot see, using processes you cannot verify, exhibiting behaviors even the vendor may not fully understand. When that model fails, you own the consequences anyway.

Speed as a force multiplier varies by orders of magnitude. Critical infrastructure operates in seconds. Healthcare operates in minutes to hours. Financial services operate in milliseconds. Each sector has a different human intervention window. AI shortens all of them. Sometimes the failure is visible only after the consequences are irreversible.

These six risk primitives are the connective tissue across every scenario, chapter, and sector that follows. You will see them repeated, recombined, and amplified. Not as a catalog of threats, but as an argument about how tightly coupled systems fail when AI becomes the connective tissue between data, decisions, and operations.

*How to Approach This Work*

Part I defines the shared problem, the convergence dynamics that apply across every sector. Read this first. It gives you the mental model every subsequent chapter builds on.

Parts II through IV translate that model into consequence. Part II covers critical infrastructure (power, water, transportation), where failure becomes safety events and cascading outages. Part III covers healthcare (diagnosis, treatment, privacy), where the system isn't mechanical but human bodies and irreversibility. Part IV covers financial services (trading, fraud, liquidity), where machine speed means the first human to notice arrives after the event has already propagated.

Part V stops being sector-by-sector and becomes cascade-by-cascade. It connects convergent pressures, governance gaps, and what responsible action looks like when incentives reward speed over safety.

You can read straight through for the full conceptual model, or start with your sector and circle back to trace shared risks. Either way, keep one practical lens throughout: underline every moment a system trusts an output it cannot independently verify. That's where convergence becomes a consequence.

The AI Convergence Trap ended with a question: whether we would build AI convergence wisely, or discover the cost through catastrophe.

The building is clearly underway; today's advances may be "incremental AI", but full AI convergence is inevitable. The question now is whether you understand both what you're standing inside and what happens when the first domino falls. Life finds a way. So does chaos. So does AI.

The question is whether you see it coming before it reaches you.

# Part I : The Common Thread

## Chapter 1: Fifteen Lines of Text

Three sectors. One vulnerability. Three wounds.

Critical infrastructure built air gaps to keep digital failures from becoming physical disasters. Healthcare built privacy walls to preserve patient autonomy. Financial services built separation of duties to contain systemic risk.

AI convergence dissolves all of them. Not through negligence or attack, but by design. The efficiency gains that justify AI adoption *require* synthesis across the silos those boundaries maintain. You cannot optimize what you cannot see. You cannot synthesize what you cannot connect.

Efficiency and fragility. Same architecture, different shadows, and you don't get to choose which one you're standing in.

The prompt injection is identical in each case. A carefully crafted input, embedded in what appears to be routine data, that hijacks the AI's instruction stream. The same technique. The same exploit. The same fifteen lines of adversarial text.

At the utility, it corrupts load-balancing recommendations. The AI begins subtly misallocating power across the grid. Operators trust the system. By the time anyone notices the cascade building, three substations are stressed beyond safe parameters.

At the hospital, it corrupts the diagnostic support system. The AI starts weighting certain symptoms toward specific diagnoses, not by chance, but by intent. Patients undergo tests for illnesses they don't have, while real conditions go unnoticed. No one sees the pattern until a malpractice attorney does.

At the bank, it infiltrates the fraud detection model. The AI begins classifying certain transaction patterns as legitimate, patterns that happen to match the attacker's exfiltration method. Millions move before the model's sudden blind spot triggers an audit.

Same vulnerability. Three wounds. This is the reality of AI convergence across these sectors: the attack surface is universal, but the bleeding is local.

*Where Boundaries Used to Be*

You can restrict access to the 'Executive Compensation' folder. You cannot restrict access to information that relates to executive compensation, the semantic neighborhood where that concept lives. You can't put a permission boundary around a region of meaning. You can't lock a gradient.

When AI systems synthesize information across traditional silos, they dissolve the access controls that took decades to build. Separation of duties, approval workflows, information classification all assume walls that AI removes by design. The walls served different purposes in each sector. The consequences of their absence differ accordingly.

In critical infrastructure, boundaries AI has rendered permeable connect operational technology to information technology in ways legacy protocols never contemplated. The Purdue model's hierarchical levels were designed to limit communication pathways. AI requires data from physical sensors, controllers, supervisory systems, and enterprise analytics simultaneously. The hierarchy becomes a mesh. The air gap becomes a suggestion.

In healthcare, walls that no longer hold enable inference attacks that patients never imagined possible. The psychiatric treatment paid for out-of-pocket specifically to keep it off insurance records? AI can reconstruct it from patterns in other care: prescription timing, appointment scheduling, referral networks. The patient consented to none of this. The AI requires no consent.

In financial services, silos AI now bridges allow correlation across products in ways that expose protected information, enable market manipulation, or trigger compliance violations across multiple regulatory regimes simultaneously. The customer who carefully managed which institution knew what discovers that AI has synthesized everything anyway.

Traditional access control asked: *who can reach which repository?* That question no longer applies. The AI is the repository. And queries to that system reveal information that no individual data source contains.

### *The Geometry of Exposure*

Traditional databases stored information in locations: a file in a folder, a record in a table. AI systems work differently. When information enters an AI, it is converted into mathematical coordinates that capture its *meaning* as a position in geometric space. Concepts that are semantically related become neighbors, regardless of how they were administratively classified. A customer complaint about billing and an internal memo about pricing policy might live in completely different systems under traditional architecture. In an AI's vector space, they cluster together because they *mean* related things.

When organizational information transforms from categorical storage to geometric representation, security implications follow from mathematics, not policy. Meaning becomes location. Related concepts cluster together in high-dimensional space. The AI navigates this space by proximity, and proximity respects no classification scheme.

A power grid AI positions "emergency shutdown procedures" geometrically close to "maintenance scheduling." A query about the latter drifts toward the former. The user never asked for emergency protocols. The geometry delivered them anyway.

A healthcare AI clusters patient conditions in ways that enable inference attacks. A query about common symptoms returns results that disclose diagnoses the patient wanted protected. The inference emerges from the space itself.

A financial AI positions trading strategies near market data. Sophisticated queries can reconstruct proprietary approaches by navigating the semantic neighborhood. No one exfiltrated the strategy. The geometry made it legible.

Your organization almost certainly lacks a map of its own semantic terrain. You cannot identify where sensitive concepts cluster, which benign queries approach them, or which trajectories through the space constitute reconnaissance. The landscape exists. Adversaries learn it. Defenders remain blind.

*Confident and Wrong*

AI hallucination, the generation of plausible falsehood with inappropriate certainty, is not a bug to be fixed. It is a mathematical property of how large language models represent knowledge. What varies is what happens when the hallucination goes undetected.

A hallucinated maintenance schedule at a utility creates equipment failures. A hallucinated diagnosis at a hospital creates unnecessary surgery, or missed disease. A hallucinated risk assessment at a bank creates exposure that compounds until someone audits the positions.

The defense mechanisms are conceptually identical: verification systems that assume hallucinations will occur, confidence calibration that prevents false precision, explainability requirements that let humans evaluate AI reasoning. The investment each sector makes in those mechanisms should reflect the damage hallucination inflicts. It rarely does. Organizations calibrate for efficiency. Consequences calibrate for physics.

Every sector faces the same governance gap: boards approving AI investments they do not understand, accountability diffusing when AI decisions cause harm, vendor relationships optimizing for capability over security. The regulatory frameworks that should provide guardrails were built for different threats. Critical infrastructure regulations assumed physical safety challenges like equipment failures, natural disasters, and human error. Financial services regulations assumed market risks and fraud patterns that humans perpetrate at human speeds. Healthcare regulations assumed privacy threats from unauthorized access, not inference attacks that reconstruct protected information from patterns no access control governs. None of these frameworks contemplated AI systems that learn, adapt, and fail in ways their designers cannot predict. Compliance with existing regulations provides false comfort. The threats have moved. The rules have not.

*When Digital Becomes Physical*

*14:23:17 EST, February 2024.*

A regional transmission operator's AI-assisted load forecasting system receives corrupted weather data from a compromised meteorological feed. The corruption is subtle. Temperature predictions shifted by a few degrees, precipitation probabilities adjusted. Traditional validation sees nothing wrong. The data looks normal.

The AI does not see normal. It sees patterns in the embedding space that match historical conditions requiring reduced generation capacity. The model adjusts predicted demand downward by 12%.

*14:27:33 EST.* Automated systems respond to the forecast. Generation capacity begins shedding. The grid, designed to balance supply and demand in real time, follows the AI's recommendations because the AI has been consistently right for months.

*14:31:44 EST.* The frequency deviation triggers protective relays across three interconnected utilities. The actual load, unchanged by the phantom weather, exceeds available generation. Equipment designed to prevent cascade failure does exactly what it was designed to do: it disconnects.

*14:48:51 EST.* Manual override completes. Seventeen minutes, an eternity in grid operations. The cascade has affected 2.3 million customers across four states.

The root cause analysis will eventually identify the attack vector: an adversarial input crafted to exploit specific embedding relationships in the forecasting model's semantic space. The weather data fooled the AI precisely because it was designed to fool the AI, not to look wrong, but to mean wrong.

The grid did what the AI told it to do. The AI did what the data told it to do. Every component worked. The system failed. This is what tight coupling means.

*Three Coupling Relationships, Three Failure Modes*

In critical infrastructure, the distance between digital decision and physical consequence is measured in seconds. AI systems controlling power grids don't just process information. They actuate. They open valves, close switches, reroute power. A compromised recommendation doesn't produce a bad report. It produces a blackout. The coupling leaves no room for human review at operational speed. By the time an operator questions the AI's recommendation, the protective relays have already fired. The seventeen minutes of manual override aren't response time. They're recovery time. The damage is done in the first thirty seconds.

Healthcare occupies different territory on the coupling spectrum. Human clinicians typically intervene between AI output and patient outcome, a buffer that provides something critical infrastructure lacks: time to question, verify, and exercise independent judgment. But the buffer is eroding. Part II traces how surgical robots, automated dispensing, and algorithmic treatment protocols are compressing decision windows from hours to minutes. Each advancement increases efficiency while eliminating a layer of defense against AI error.

Financial services operate with the loosest physical coupling. AI decisions move money, not molecules. A trading algorithm's error doesn't physically harm anyone in the immediate moment. But financial systems' interconnections create a different kind of consequence. Errors propagate through markets, institutions, and economies in ways that infrastructure failures do not. The 2010 Flash Crash, when algorithmic trading contributed to a thousand-point Dow drop in minutes, demonstrated how quickly AI-adjacent failures cascade through financial systems. The danger in financial services isn't the immediate physical consequence. It's the systemic interdependence: the way failures at one institution propagate to counterparties, the way correlated AI behaviors create correlated failures, the way speed that exceeds human cognition removes the possibility of human intervention.

Critical infrastructure security must design fail-safe defaults that revert to safe states when AI fails or behaves unexpectedly. Healthcare security must design for transparency, making AI's role visible to clinicians who can exercise independent judgment. Financial services security must design circuit breakers that halt cascading failures before they propagate through interconnected systems.

All three require anomaly detection that catches AI failures before they manifest as physical, clinical, or financial consequences. The metrics differ. The thresholds differ. The response procedures differ. The underlying reality does not: when digital systems couple to physical consequences, the security architecture must account for what happens when those systems fail.

They will fail. The only question is what breaks when they do.

# Chapter 2: The Inheritance

A typical power utility's control room is an archaeological site. Mechanical relays from the 1970s still click through operations their designers never imagined would persist half a century later. Programmable logic controllers from the 1980s run code written in ladder logic by engineers who have long since retired. Supervisory Control and Data Acquisition (SCADA) systems from the 1990s supervise these devices through interfaces designed before "cyber" meant anything to operational engineers. Distributed control systems from the 2000s sit uneasily alongside their purely operational predecessors. And now, Internet of Things (IoT) sensors from the 2010s stream data to analytics platforms promising optimization through machine learning.

This isn't interesting. It's determinative. Every AI integration into critical infrastructure must contend with this inheritance: systems designed for different assumptions about connectivity, security, and operational tempo. You cannot greenfield a power grid. You cannot shut down a water treatment plant to modernize it. Every enhancement must work alongside systems that predate the protocols, interfaces, and security models that modern AI assumes.

The oldest systems operate in a world of continuous physical signals: electromechanical relays, analog instrumentation, hardwired controls. They have no concept of data packets, network addresses, or authentication. They cannot be "upgraded" to speak digital protocols because there is nothing to upgrade; their operation is analog. These systems persist because they are reliable, because their failure modes are well understood, and because replacing them requires physical access to substations, treatment plants, and control centers scattered across vast geographies.

The next generation, which comprised early digital systems from the 1980s and 1990s, introduced programmable logic but retained the assumption of physical isolation. Modbus, developed in 1979, transmits data without encryption, authentication, or integrity verification. Distributed Network Protocol 3 (DNP3), developed specifically for utilities, added reliability features but still assumed physical network isolation provided adequate security. IEC 61850 offers authentication capabilities that most deployments don't use because the underlying systems can't support them. These protocols weren't designed carelessly. They were designed for environments where physical isolation provided security. A Modbus device behind a locked substation fence, connected only to other devices behind similar fences, didn't need cryptographic authentication. The attacker who could intercept those communications had already breached the physical security that was the only safeguard that mattered.

AI convergence demands connectivity these assumptions cannot accommodate. Machine learning requires data from across the operational environment. The AI system optimizing a power grid needs real-time information about generation, transmission, distribution, and demand. This data cannot flow across air gaps. It requires exactly the connectivity that traditional Operational Technology (OT) security was designed to prevent. Every connection created for AI integration becomes a potential attack vector: a new pathway between the physical world and the digital systems that increasingly govern it.

We have programmable logic controllers (PLCs) running code that was compiled before some of our junior engineers were born, a grid operations manager at a major Midwestern utility observes. The vendor that made them doesn't exist anymore. The engineer who wrote the logic retired in 2003. But those controllers still work, every day, reliably. And now someone wants to feed their data into an AI model that will 'optimize' operations. I ask them: what happens when the optimization is wrong? They don't have a good answer. Neither do I. That's what keeps me up at night.

Nation-state adversaries target critical infrastructure persistently, and each convergence step hands them new entry points.

*Three Sectors, Three Histories*

Healthcare's legacy systems reflect a different history: the digitization of patient records, the proliferation of specialized clinical applications, the complex integration requirements of modern medical practice. The electronic health record systems that dominate American healthcare are Epic, Cerner, and Meditech. They were designed as comprehensive clinical platforms, not as AI integration substrates. They assume human users navigating structured interfaces, not AI systems synthesizing information across patient populations. The Application Programming Interface (API)'s they expose were designed for specific use cases: connecting lab systems, enabling patient portals, transmitting prescriptions. Not for the comprehensive synthesis AI convergence requires.

Electronic Health Record (EHR) systems encode access controls in ways that don't translate to AI contexts. A nurse's access to view patient records during a shift does not map to an AI system's access to synthesize those records for population health analysis. The consent frameworks embedded in these systems assume specific human-to-human information flows, not AI-mediated synthesis. Medical device integration adds another layer. The Food and Drug Administration (FDA)-regulated devices must maintain their approved security postures even when integrated with AI systems. A patient monitor feeding data to an AI analysis platform creates a chain of devices with different regulatory statuses, different vendor support arrangements, and different security update cycles. Managing this heterogeneity while maintaining patient safety requires governance frameworks that do not yet exist in mature forms.

Financial services appear to have the least burdensome legacy inheritance. Banks have led technology adoption for decades. This apparent advantage conceals significant technical debt that AI convergence exposes. Major financial institutions run core systems originally built in COBOL during the 1960s and 1970s. These systems process millions of transactions daily with reliability rates that modern systems struggle to match. They embed business logic that no living employee fully understands, documentation that may be incomplete or lost, interfaces that assume batch processing rather than real-time AI integration.

The challenge is not that these systems are bad. They are sturdy. The challenge is that they were designed for a world of discrete transactions, clear audit trails, and human-speed processing. AI convergence demands synthesis across these systems in ways their designers never contemplated. The patterns that emerge from cross-system analysis may reveal relationships that existing audit mechanisms cannot track. Decades of compliance requirements have created audit and reporting infrastructure that assumes specific data structures, transaction patterns, and decision processes. Because these AI systems reason through probabilistic inference rather than deterministic rules, they may produce compliant outcomes through non-compliant processes. The audit trail shows the decision. It cannot show how the decision emerged from patterns no human specified.

Three sectors. Three different histories. One shared reality: the systems society cannot live without were built by people who could not imagine what we would ask those systems to become. The engineers who wrote the ladder logic are gone. The architects who designed the EHR workflows have moved on. The COBOL programmers who encoded the business rules have retired or died. What remains is infrastructure: load-bearing walls in institutional architecture that AI must work around, work with, or work through. There is no clean slate. There is only inheritance.

*The Adversaries Who Wait*

Your utility might employ dozens of security professionals. An intelligence agency focused on it might deploy hundreds. You must defend every potential attack vector. The adversary needs to find only one. This asymmetry defines the threat landscape for critical infrastructure. And AI convergence makes it worse.

Four nation-states account for the overwhelming majority of state-sponsored cyber activity targeting critical infrastructure: Russia, China, Iran, and North Korea. Each brings different capabilities. All bring resources that individual utilities cannot match.

Russian actors have demonstrated the most consequential attacks on power systems to date. The December 2015 and December 2016 attacks on Ukrainian distribution companies required deep understanding of operational technology, custom malware development, and coordination across multiple stages. The attackers didn't just compromise computers. They operated the human-machine interfaces that controlled the grid, opening breakers and disconnecting load while preventing remote recovery. Russian targeting extends well beyond Ukraine. U.S. intelligence assessments indicate persistent reconnaissance of American grid infrastructure, including access to systems that could be used for future attacks.

Chinese operations pursue different objectives with different methods. The goal appears to be positioning for potential future conflict rather than current disruption. Chinese actors have compromised utilities, transportation systems, and communications infrastructure, though typically for reconnaissance and access maintenance rather than destructive attacks. This access-focused strategy may be more dangerous than Russia's occasional demonstrations. Chinese actors have shown patience measured in years, maintaining persistent presence in compromised networks without taking actions that would reveal their access. The scale of this presence is difficult to assess.

Discovered incidents represent only a fraction of actual access. The access obtained may sit dormant for years. The intelligence collected may inform planning for contingencies that may never occur. The capabilities developed may never be used, or may be used decisively in some future crisis that current planning cannot anticipate.

Iran and North Korea bring their own capabilities to the landscape, less sophisticated than Russia or China in most respects but persistent and increasingly capable, particularly in ransomware operations and sanctions evasion through cyber means.

AI convergence creates new opportunities for these patient adversaries. An AI system synthesizing data across previously isolated control systems provides a single target whose compromise affects multiple capabilities. An AI system trained on operational data might be poisoned to make systematically poor decisions during crisis conditions, the high-stress periods when operators depend on it most. The vulnerability introduced today might be exploited years hence. Security for AI convergence in critical infrastructure must account for threats that may not manifest for years. The adversaries operate on strategic timescales, not fiscal years.

*The Healthcare Mosaic*

Healthcare faces a more diverse threat landscape. Nation-states target healthcare for intelligence: stealing pharmaceutical research, gathering data for espionage, probing pandemic response capabilities. But healthcare's most frequent adversaries are criminal organizations seeking financial gain.

Healthcare data commands premium prices on criminal markets. A single patient record that contains identity information, insurance data, and medical history enables multiple fraud schemes. Unlike credit card numbers, which can be changed, medical histories are permanent. The value persists indefinitely. Ransomware has proven devastatingly effective. Hospitals cannot go offline while systems recover; patients continue arriving, procedures continue being needed. The operational pressure to restore service creates leverage that attackers in other sectors rarely achieve.

AI convergence amplifies both the value of healthcare data to attackers and the consequences of successful attacks. AI systems that synthesize information across patient populations create single points of exposure. AI systems that inform clinical decisions become targets whose compromise affects patient care directly.

September 2024. A regional health system's clinical decision support AI begins recommending subtly elevated medication dosages. The deviation is within acceptable ranges, at the higher end of published guidelines. The poisoning occurred three months earlier, when training data was compromised during a routine model update. By the time patterns emerge in adverse event reporting, 847 patients have received affected recommendations. Determining causation will take years. The liability exposure is incalculable.

The chief medical information officer, reviewing the incident timeline: We had logging. We had access controls. We had change management. None of it was designed for this.

*The Fraud Ecosystem*

Financial fraud is not an opportunistic crime. It is an organized enterprise with its own supply chains, specialization, and continuous innovation. This ecosystem adapts to defensive improvements with remarkable speed. You patch Tuesday; they pivot Wednesday. When financial institutions deployed machine learning for fraud detection, fraudsters began using machine learning to evade detection. The arms race is already underway.

Deepfake technology enables impersonation attacks at scale. A Hong Kong finance worker transferred $25 million after joining a video call whose apparent company executives were all AI-generated deepfakes. The attack succeeded because it combined multiple seemingly independent verifications: the request came from known contacts, in a familiar meeting format, with multiple apparent participants. Each element reinforced the others' apparent legitimacy. AI-generated phishing, customized for individual targets based on synthesized information, achieves success rates that generic phishing never could. The messages reference actual projects, use language patterns matching legitimate correspondents, and arrive at psychologically optimal times. Reconnaissance that once took weeks now runs automatically.

Nation-states also target financial services, though with different objectives. Sanctions evasion, market manipulation, intelligence collection. North Korea's cyber operations have stolen billions in cryptocurrency and traditional currency to fund state programs. The financial services threat landscape combines the most sophisticated criminal operations, nation-state strategic objectives, and insider threats from employees with access to high-value systems. AI convergence provides new tools to all parties in an already intense conflict.

# Chapter 3: The Forgetting

The compliance officer stares at the incident report, then at the North American Electric Reliability Corporation Critical Infrastructure Protection (NERC CIP) checklist on her desk. Every box is checked. Every control is documented. The utility passed its last audit with zero findings.

The AI system that just failed isn't mentioned anywhere in the standards.

NERC CIP assumes deterministic systems with clear boundaries. AI convergence dissolves exactly that. The regulations specify access controls for defined perimeters. They mandate logging for discrete transactions. They require human oversight of identified critical functions. The attack didn't cross a perimeter. It navigated semantic space. The transaction it corrupted wasn't discrete. It was a synthesis across six data sources the regulations never contemplated connecting. The human who was supposed to provide oversight trusted an AI recommendation that emerged from processes no audit framework knows how to examine.

*Full compliance. Complete exposure.*

These three sectors exist on a regulatory spectrum that creates its own fragility. Critical infrastructure operates with light federal cybersecurity oversight. Healthcare layers HIPAA atop FDA device regulations, state laws, professional licensing, and accreditation standards: dense coverage that creates compliance burden without addressing AI. Financial services is neck-deep in oversight: SEC, OCC, FDIC, FINRA, CFPB, the Federal Reserve, state regulators, plus SR 11-7 model risk requirements, Basel frameworks, and a dozen international jurisdictions with conflicting demands. The most regulated sector in the American economy, wrapped in compliance infrastructure that other industries cannot imagine, and none of it designed for AI.

The asymmetry matters for cascades. Financial services have governance frameworks that can be extended to AI contexts, imperfectly but genuinely. Critical infrastructure has gaps where that infrastructure should be. When AI failures cascade from the least-governed sector into the most-governed ones, the regulatory density downstream cannot compensate for the regulatory vacuum upstream. The grid doesn't answer to twelve jurisdictions. It barely answers to one. And everything else depends on it.

*The Grid's Invisible Gap*

The electric power sector operates under the most developed cybersecurity regulatory framework in critical infrastructure. NERC CIP standards are prescriptive: they specify required controls rather than requiring "adequate" security. This precision creates clarity about what compliance means. It also creates precision about what compliance doesn't cover.

The standards assume systems behave predictably. They assume information stays where it's put. They assume boundaries exist to be defended. AI convergence violates every assumption. When a grid operator deploys AI for load forecasting, the AI synthesizes weather data, historical patterns, economic indicators, and real-time sensor feeds into predictions that inform operational decisions. NERC CIP tells you how to protect the sensor feeds. It says nothing about protecting the synthesis. Nor about detecting when that synthesis has been subtly corrupted.

The gap isn't regulatory negligence. It's temporal inevitability. Regulations follow incidents. The incidents that will shape AI-specific grid requirements haven't happened yet, or haven't been recognized for what they were. Water systems face the same structural lag. TSA pipeline requirements, written after Colonial Pipeline went dark, address the attack that already occurred. Neither framework anticipates how AI changes what "the system" even means.

*The Patchwork That Doesn't Cover*

Healthcare operates under perhaps the most complex regulatory environment of any American industry. HIPAA provides the federal floor. State laws add walls. FDA device regulations overlay everything. Accreditation standards demand their own compliance. This density creates an illusion of coverage. Surely, with so many frameworks, something addresses AI security. Almost nothing does.

HIPAA's Privacy and Security Rules assume specific data flows: a covered entity shares information with a business associate under contractual protections. The rules map onto a world of discrete transactions between identified parties. AI synthesis breaks this model at every joint. When AI combines de-identified datasets in ways that re-identify patients, which entity violated which rule? When model weights encode protected health information in mathematical representations the regulations never contemplated, is the information "disclosed" or "stored" or something the law has no name for?

The FDA regulates AI that qualifies as a medical device, a category that expands faster than the agency can define it. The Software as a Medical Device framework accommodates AI's continuous learning, acknowledging that the system deployed today may behave differently next month. But "accommodate" is not "govern." The frameworks remain works in progress applied to systems already in production. State laws add complexity without coverage: some mandate AI-specific disclosures while professional licensing requirements constrain what decisions AI can influence, but the constraints assume someone knows which decisions AI influenced, a determination increasingly difficult to make.

The patchwork covers the terrain regulators mapped years ago. AI operates in territory the maps don't show.

*Twelve Jurisdictions, Zero Answers*

A global bank's AI system trains on data from Frankfurt, processes it through models refined in Singapore, runs on infrastructure hosted in Virginia, and serves customers across forty-three countries. The system is coherent. The regulatory landscape is not.

The EU AI Act classifies financial services AI as "high-risk," triggering conformity assessments and human oversight mandates that continue evolving. The United States fragments authority across a half-dozen federal agencies, none coordinating AI oversight with the others. SR 11-7 model risk management guidance, the most developed regulatory approach to AI in finance, was written before transformer architectures existed. Regulators are extending it to AI contexts, but extension is interpretation, and interpretation varies by examiner.

Then come the requirements that conflict directly. Fair lending laws demand explainable credit decisions. GDPR grants rights to meaningful information about algorithmic processing. The regulatory expectation that decisions trace to specific factors doesn't map onto systems whose "factors" are mathematical weights distributed across billions of parameters.

"*The regulators want us to explain why the model denied a loan,*" a chief compliance officer observes. "*The honest answer is: because of complex interactions across hundreds of features weighted through processes we cannot decompose into human-interpretable logic. That's not an answer they can accept. So we generate post-hoc explanations that sound reasonable, knowing they're approximations at best: fictions we tell to satisfy requirements that assume decisions work the way they used to work.*"

The lag between what frameworks require and what AI convergence creates is structural, not temporary. It compounds every quarter. No compliance checklist names prompt injection attacks, model poisoning, or adversarial manipulation. The rules don't reach where you're operating. Build as if they never will.

This is the compliance mirage: the appearance of oversight where oversight cannot actually occur. It recurs across every sector this book examines: from the CIP auditor who passes the utility on controls that don't cover AI, to the bank examiner who reviews model governance that no one understands, to the healthcare accreditor who certifies processes designed for a world that no longer exists. Recognize the shape: full compliance, complete exposure. You will see it repeated in every section that follows.

*The Last People Who Remember*

The compliance officer wasn't describing a technology problem. She was describing the systematic elimination of the last redundancy every complex system depends on: humans who remember why things are built the way they are.

Boeing didn't crash two planes because engineers made mistakes. They crashed because the engineers who would have caught the mistakes were gone, replaced by cheaper labor, pushed out in pursuit of efficiency, their institutional knowledge treated as overhead rather than infrastructure. The people who understood which edge cases were dangerous, which redundancies mattered, which shortcuts could kill, they weren't in the room when MCAS was approved.

AI convergence is creating conditions for the same slow-motion failure across all three sectors. Not through malice. Through forgetting.

The expertise gap isn't that people lack credentials. It's that the credentials don't exist. Critical infrastructure needs professionals who understand operational technology, AI systems, and their intersection. Almost no training program produces this combination. The knowledge lives in people who've spent decades in control rooms. When they retire, it retires with them. No documentation captures why the veteran operator glances at a specific gauge whenever load forecasting seems off. The AI doesn't know to glance. The new operators don't know why they should.

Healthcare needs professionals who understand clinical workflows, patient safety, regulatory requirements, and AI systems simultaneously. Financial services appears better positioned: it has used quantitative methods longest and pays for talent. But traditional quant skills don't translate to AI security. Every sector faces the same fundamental problem: AI convergence demands expertise that doesn't exist in sufficient quantity, arriving faster than any training pipeline can produce it. The gap between what you are deploying and what your people understand widens with every deployment cycle.

*The Forgetting*

Institutional knowledge rarely lives in documentation. It lives in people who remember why certain systems were never connected, why a control exists that looks inefficient, why an exception was carved out after a fraud incident ten years ago. When those people leave, the control remains. Its rationale disappears. Someone eventually removes it to "streamline operations." The wound reopens.

Critical infrastructure will be slowest, because physical operations require presence, and operators who've worked the same systems for decades provide continuity no AI can replace. But transformation is coming even here. The expertise erosion will be gradual, invisible until the day an AI recommendation seems plausible and no one in the room remembers why it's wrong.

Healthcare will forget selectively. Diagnostic specialties watch AI approach and exceed human performance in narrow domains. The radiologist who's spent twenty years learning which shadows matter: what happens when that person's role reduces to reviewing AI recommendations, then to auditing AI outputs, then to providing legal cover for AI decisions? The expertise doesn't just change. It atrophies. Muscles unused grow weak.

Financial services will forget the fastest and most completely. The sector is databases with humans attached. The displacement has already begun: trading floors that once employed thousands now operate with dozens of humans overseeing automated systems. The most dangerous consequence isn't the knowledge that walks out the door. It's the control someone removes because no one remembers what it was protecting against.

If you preserve human judgment as genuine redundancy, not performance, not theater, but actual capacity to catch what AI misses, you will navigate AI convergence with resilience. Those that eliminate humans faster than they can transfer institutional knowledge will discover what Boeing discovered: the last redundancy was never optional. It was the only thing standing between confidence and catastrophe.

What that catastrophe looks like, when the expertise is gone and the systems fail together, is not abstract. It is a specific sequence of events, unfolding across sectors, faster than anyone can respond.

# Chapter 4: The Dominoes

The AI managing grid load across three states receives corrupted sensor data at 2:47 AM. It responds the way it was trained to respond: adjusting power flow to match what it believes demand requires. The adjustments are wrong. Cascading failures begin propagating through the interconnection.

By 2:52 AM, the first hospital loses primary power. Backup generators activate. They are designed to carry critical systems for seventy-two hours. No one expects to need them that long.

By 3:15 AM, the regional financial clearing system detects anomalies. Transactions are failing. Backup links to alternate data centers require power the backup systems weren't designed to provide indefinitely. Risk management systems begin flagging positions they can no longer validate.

By 4:30 AM, a second hospital loses generator fuel. The fuel delivery company's dispatch system runs on servers in a data center that lost power ninety minutes ago. Manual workarounds require phone calls to drivers whose phones route through cellular towers now operating on battery backup.

By dawn, what failed no longer matters; what still works does.

*The Floor Beneath Everything*

Healthcare and financial services exist because critical infrastructure exists. Hospitals cannot operate without power. Trading cannot execute without telecommunications. The electronic systems defining modern medicine and finance function only because electricity flows, networks connect, and transportation moves. This dependency is so fundamental it becomes invisible, until it isn't.

An AI-related failure in the power grid doesn't just affect utilities. It affects every hospital whose backup power eventually depletes, every pharmacy whose refrigeration fails, every patient on home medical equipment that requires electricity. It affects every financial institution whose trading systems go dark, every ATM that stops dispensing cash, every payment processor whose transactions fail.

The cascade runs in every direction. A financial system failure that disrupts payment processing affects utilities that need to pay employees and suppliers. A healthcare system failure that overwhelms regional capacity affects the financial institutions whose employees can't work because they're caring for family members the system can't treat. A transportation failure that halts fuel delivery affects hospitals whose generators require diesel, banks whose armored vehicles can't reach branches, power plants whose coal trains never arrive.

AI convergence amplifies these dependencies because it connects what was once separate. The AI systems managing grid operations synthesize data from sources across sectors: weather data, economic indicators, even healthcare utilization patterns that affect regional energy demand. Every connection that improves efficiency creates a new pathway for failure to propagate.

Healthcare and financial services intertwine through relationships most people never see. Health insurers are financial institutions operating in healthcare contexts. Their AI systems price risk using clinical data, demographic information, and claims histories that span both sectors. Healthcare providers depend on capital markets for financing. Building facilities, purchasing equipment, and maintaining operations require access to credit, which requires functioning financial systems.

Medical debt is a financial product following financial services dynamics. The AI systems that manage collections, price receivables, and securitize payment streams operate in a space where healthcare and finance become indistinguishable. AI convergence in healthcare affects financial services. Hospital AI that optimizes capacity affects the utilization data insurers use to set premiums. Clinical AI that predicts patient outcomes influences the investment calculations that determine which healthcare organizations receive capital. AI systems that synthesize information across both sectors, which analyze health data alongside financial data for risk assessment, create joint vulnerabilities neither sector's regulatory framework addresses. The attack surface isn't healthcare or finance. It's the space where they connect.

If you have read straight through, you have already seen this cascade in outline and then in summary. What follows is the full resolution. If you entered through your sector, what follows is why the rest of the book exists.

The data poisoning began eleven weeks earlier: subtle corruption of the sensor feeds the grid's AI trusted most heavily, drifting its model of actual conditions so gradually that the divergence looked like seasonal variation. No one noticed. The AI compensated. That was the point.

*02:47:11 CST, Tuesday, October 28.* A cold front pushes demand above forecast across the northern service territory. Routine. The AI responds with adjustments calibrated to conditions it believes exist. The conditions are wrong. The adjustments make everything worse.

Carlos Reyes, senior grid operator, nineteen years on the floor, sees voltage sag on the 345kV Corridor West line. He reaches for the phone.

*02:48:33 CST.* The AI reads the sag as a demand signal and pushes additional load through the same corridor. Protective relays trip at Corridor West. The AI interprets the isolation as a generation shortfall and redistributes load across adjacent substations already running near thermal limits it does not accurately perceive. Mill Creek trips. Then Ridgeview.

*02:51:44 CST.* Reyes and two colleagues attempt manual override. The SCADA interface accepts their commands, but the AI's optimization layer keeps issuing competing instructions through a parallel control path. It was added during last year's modernization, which was documented in a vendor specification none of them had read. The switchgear receives conflicting signals.

*02:52:19 CST.* St. Raphael Medical Center, a 340-bed trauma center forty miles south, loses primary power. Generators start within eight seconds. Rachel Okafor, night nursing supervisor, notes the time and calls facilities. Generators are running normally. She returns to shift handoff.

*02:53:41 CST.* Three hundred miles east, Meridian Capital, a clearing firm settling for eleven regional banks, flags a connectivity anomaly. Latency spikes from 4 milliseconds to 340. The AI reroutes settlement queues through backup links. David Park, overnight risk analyst, confirms rerouting. He does not yet know the backup links terminate in a facility drawing power from the same failing grid.

*02:58:22 CST.* Reyes regains manual control. The AI is disconnected. But seventeen minutes of misallocation have stressed equipment across the interconnection. Field crews are dispatched to verify substations. The dispatch system runs on cellular towers now on battery backup rated for four hours.

*03:17:00 CST.* Park's dashboard turns red. Backup settlement links are degrading. Transactions are timing out. The AI retry logic is generating duplicate submissions that the receiving systems, themselves degraded, accept only intermittently. Some transactions are settling twice. The confirmation feeds Park relies on are now fourteen minutes stale. He calls his supervisor at home. The call takes three attempts.

*03:34:08 CST.* St. Raphael's pharmacy system requires network connectivity to verify controlled substance dispensing against the state prescription monitoring database. The connection is intermittent. The AI queues requests rather than dispensing without confirmation. That is the correct safety behavior. A patient in the Emergency Department (ED) with a fractured femur waits eleven minutes for pain medication while pharmacist James Watanabe fights through two failed authentication attempts on a cellular network running on battery backup.

*03:47:00 CST.* Rachel Okafor asks facilities to confirm the fuel resupply timeline. The distributor's dispatch system is hosted in a data center that lost power an hour ago. The call doesn't connect. The generators have fuel for days. But the question has been asked, and it has no answer.

*05:00:00 CST.* Three of the eleven banks Meridian clears for have AI fraud systems flagging the duplicate transactions as fraud, not system errors. Automated holds are freezing legitimate transactions. The fraud detection is working as designed. It is making everything worse.

*07:00:00 CST.* Markets open on data feeds ranging from current to four hours stale. AI risk platforms generate position reports mixing accurate and inaccurate settlement data. Decisions are being made on numbers that are wrong in ways nobody has yet mapped.

*12:00:00 CST.* Power restored to 94% of customers. St. Raphael is back on primary. But six morning surgeries were delayed. A 71-year-old with a cardiac valve replacement scheduled for 7:30

AM has been sent home and told to return Thursday. His cardiologist charts the delay as an "administrative scheduling adjustment." The chart will not mention a corrupted sensor feed in another state.

Carlos Reyes finishes a fourteen-hour shift. In his incident log, under root cause, he writes: *"All automated responses were consistent with training. Cascade resulted from correct system behavior under incorrect conditions."*

Every component worked. The system failed.

*What No Organization Controls*

The cascade scenario isn't hypothetical. Every element has occurred separately: grid attacks, hospital generator failures, financial system outages, telecommunications degradation. These elements will combine. The only question is when.

No individual utility, hospital, or bank, yours included, can secure the interdependent systems on which they all depend. A hospital that hardens its own AI systems remains vulnerable to grid AI failures. A bank that perfects its incident response can't function if telecommunications fail. A utility that detects and blocks attacks on its systems can't prevent cascades that originate elsewhere. The threat isn't to sectors. It's to the connections between them.

Information sharing becomes a security necessity, not a compliance checkbox. The threat intelligence a utility develops about adversaries probing grid AI systems is relevant to every hospital and bank depending on that grid. The fraud patterns financial institutions detect may signal attacks that will target healthcare billing. The anomalies healthcare systems notice in AI behavior may reflect broader adversary campaigns. But sharing requires trust, standards, and mechanisms that don't yet exist at the scale interdependency demands. The Information Sharing and Analysis Centers and regulatory frameworks and government partnerships that enable coordination within sectors haven't adapted to threats that cross sectoral boundaries through AI systems designed to synthesize information from everywhere.

The organizations that engage with these coordination mechanisms, imperfect as they are, position themselves for resilience they cannot achieve alone. Those that operate in isolation face risks they cannot even see, let alone manage.

Somewhere right now, an adversary is mapping the connections between sectors, identifying the AI systems that bridge critical infrastructure and healthcare, healthcare and finance, finance and infrastructure. They understand the attack surface better than the defenders do. The dominoes are already touching.

Resist the temptation to treat AI security as a problem for later. Later is now. Every scenario in the preceding pages reflects either documented incidents or capabilities that adversaries possess today. The AI systems being deployed this quarter create the security challenges examined here.

The organizations that will manage this transformation successfully are not those that have solved the hard problems. They are those that understand waiting for solutions means waiting while vulnerabilities compound. The gap between what you're deploying and what you're prepared to defend grows wider each quarter. Into that gap flow adversaries who understand your attack surface at least as well as those who created it.

What follows examines three sectors where AI convergence creates the most acute security challenges: critical infrastructure, where failures kill; healthcare, where failures harm individuals one at a time; and financial services, where failures cascade through systems moving faster than human perception.

The sector analyses will identify tensions that have no clean resolutions, tradeoffs where reasonable people disagree, and risks that can only be managed, never eliminated, with varying degrees of skill and luck. Some tensions remain unresolved not because analysis has failed but because resolution is not available.

That discomfort is not a flaw in the analysis. It is the analysis.

We are mapping terrain that continues to shift, facing adversaries that continue to adapt, deploying technologies that continue to surprise us. The only adequate response is continuous vigilance: not because vigilance guarantees safety, but because its absence guarantees failure.

# Part II : Critical Infrastructure

## Chapter 5: When The Lights Go Out

On a cold February evening in 2021, millions of Texans discovered what happens when critical infrastructure fails.

The Electric Reliability Council of Texas (ERCOT) grid, operating independently from the two major interconnections serving the rest of the country, collapsed under Winter Storm Uri. Rolling blackouts became sustained outages. Natural gas plants failed because they lacked winterization. Wind turbines froze. The cascading failures left 4.5 million homes without power for days, killed over 200 people, and caused an estimated $195 billion in damage.

The Texas grid failure was not an AI failure. It was a failure of planning, investment, and regulatory oversight. Critical infrastructure security is continuous risk management, not a one-time perimeter defense. The biggest failures come from assumptions that the environment is closed, simple, or already covered by existing tools and policies. Texas assumed the historical range of winter conditions was sufficient. That assumption killed over 200 people. The failure establishes what AI convergence puts at risk: systems society cannot function without. When power fails, hospitals go dark. When water treatment fails, cities sicken. When transportation fails, supply chains halt.

Part I traced AI convergence in enterprise systems: damage measured in dollars, careers, competitive position. Part II traces convergence in systems where failure is measured in bodies.

Power grids, water treatment, and transportation networks share characteristics that make AI convergence both more valuable and more dangerous than anywhere else: they cannot tolerate downtime, they operate on physical timescales software cannot pause, and their failure cascades through everything that depends on them.

If you're responsible for these systems, you've spent decades building resilience through storms, equipment failures, and deliberate attack. You understand what it means to operate systems that cannot fail. Whether that understanding survives the pressure to converge is the real question.

*The Seconds Between Decision and Consequence*

AI systems in critical infrastructure actuate physical systems. A compromised AI in financial services produces bad reports. A compromised AI in a power grid opens switches. The time between decision and physical consequence is measured in seconds.

Consider an AI managing voltage regulation that receives corrupted sensor data. It doesn't flag an anomaly for human review—it adjusts transformer tap settings, opens capacitor banks, modifies power flows across transmission lines carrying enough electricity to arc through air and vaporize copper. The adjustment might be correct. Or it might cascade into equipment damage, injuries, deaths. The AI doesn't know the difference.

This tight coupling creates constraints AI enthusiasts underestimate. Through decades of blackouts and near-misses, you've learned that systems which cannot tolerate downtime require defensive depth no software architecture provides alone. Graceful degradation isn't aspirational here: it's what keeps cities alive when systems fail.

If you understand this, you're building AI integration that preserves human override, maintains manual fallback, and assumes the model will eventually be wrong about something that matters. The utilities that don't are discovering consequences the way Texas did: through catastrophic failure no retrospective analysis can undo.

*The Archaeology of Control*

The inheritance from Chapter 2, mechanical relays from the 1970s clicking alongside IoT sensors streaming to Machine Learning (ML) platforms, is the system you operate. The protocols that assumed physical isolation. The documentation never written. The engineers who retired with knowledge no one captured. These are not sector-wide observations but the constraints shaping every AI deployment decision you make.

*What Nobody Wrote Down*

Systems installed decades ago often lack complete documentation. The engineers who built them are gone. Original vendors have been merged, acquired, bankrupted. The institutional knowledge about why specific configurations exist has dispersed like dust. This void matters for AI integration.

Machine learning reflects whatever patterns exist in training data: undocumented workarounds, legacy configurations, and historical accidents no one remembers. An AI optimizing grid operations might learn to avoid certain switching sequences without anyone understanding those sequences were prohibited after a near-miss incident thirty years ago. The prohibition persists. The documentation is gone.

Why is this subnet isolated? Why does this controller require manual confirmation for certain commands? Why are these two systems never connected simultaneously?

The answers often exist only in the memories of long-tenured operators. Sometimes not even there: the original reasons predate current staff entirely.

AI systems cannot learn what has never been recorded. They optimize based on available data. When that data excludes hard-won lessons embedded in undocumented practices, optimization undoes protections that took decades to evolve.

*The People Between*

*"We've got forty-year veterans who can hear something wrong in a substation from a quarter mile away, and twenty-five-year-old data scientists who can build you a neural network in an afternoon. Getting them to speak the same language is the hardest problem I've got."*

— Director of Grid Modernization, Midwestern ISO

The engineers who understand operational technology (relay settings, protection schemes, the failure modes decades of experience revealed) rarely have AI expertise. The data scientists who understand AI rarely have OT backgrounds. The intersection barely exists.

OT engineers learned their craft in substations and control rooms. They understand why certain practices exist because they've seen what happens when those practices are violated. Their knowledge is embodied in reflexes, intuitions, unstated assumptions no training program can fully transfer.

AI engineers bring different expertise: statistical learning, model architecture, data pipeline design. They can optimize for any objective function, but specifying the right objective function requires operational knowledge they lack. The AI that optimizes for efficiency may compromise safety margins no one thought to encode as constraints.

Bridging this gap requires training OT engineers in AI or training AI engineers in OT. Both paths take years. Neither is happening at scale.

*The Gap That Was Never There*

The uranium enrichment centrifuges at Iran's Natanz facility sat behind an air gap: complete physical separation from any network an attacker could reach. No firewall to configure, no patches to apply, no authentication to manage.

Stuxnet crossed anyway.

The malware traveled on infected USB drives carried by engineers who needed to update systems that couldn't update themselves. It exploited not a network vulnerability but human behavior: maintenance. The air gap was never as solid as it seemed. The systems that couldn't connect still needed people who could.

Even before Stuxnet, air gaps were eroding. Utilities wanted remote access for monitoring. Vendors required connectivity for support. Business systems needed operational data for billing and optimization. Each connection, individually justified, collectively undermined the isolation air gaps promised.

AI convergence accelerates this erosion. Machine learning requires continuous, real-time data from across the operational environment. The AI optimizing a power grid needs information about generation, transmission, distribution, and demand. It needs historical data for training and ongoing data for adaptation. This data cannot flow across air gaps.

Your choice isn't whether to connect. It's how to survive the connection. That choice was made for you years ago.

The lesson of Stuxnet is not that air gaps are worthless. It's that every security assumption carries hidden dependencies. The transition from isolated to connected systems creates the kind of window adversaries are trained to exploit. AI convergence doesn't just open that window. It removes the wall.

The assumption that the environment was closed. That assumption proved false.

*The Hierarchy That Can't Hold*

The Purdue Enterprise Reference Architecture organized industrial control networks into levels running from physical process at the bottom to enterprise network at the top, with controlled connections between them. Communications flowed up and down in predictable patterns; requests passed through defined interfaces at each level.

AI doesn't respect these boundaries.

An AI optimizing generation dispatch needs information from physical sensors, controllers, supervisory systems, and market data. This optimization might occur in cloud infrastructure outside the Purdue hierarchy entirely. Information that never needed to leave Level 2 now flows to analytics platforms in Level 4 or the cloud. Commands that should originate from Level 3 incorporate AI recommendations from beyond the hierarchy. The neat levels become a mesh of connections the model was never designed to accommodate.

The Purdue principles of defense in depth and controlled communication remain valuable. But no consensus framework for AI-era OT/IT security has emerged. You're building from incomplete blueprints.

Every connection created for AI integration becomes a potential attack vector. Colonial Pipeline illustrated this before most AI deployments existed. Attackers compromised IT systems through a legacy Virtual Private Network (VPN) account, never breaching operational technology directly. But uncertainty about lateral movement led Colonial to shut down operations for six days. Fuel supplies across the Eastern United States disrupted. Gas stations ran dry.

Colonial's IT and OT were more separated than AI convergence requires. They shut down voluntarily because they couldn't be certain attackers hadn't reached operational systems. In a converged environment where AI systems bridge IT and OT, the pathways for lateral movement multiply. The AI platform with legitimate access to both domains creates the bridge attackers need.

Compromise the AI system and you gain influence over every decision it informs, from grid operations at scale to chemical dosing across an entire water system. The AI platform becomes the highest-value target on the network.

*Building for a World Without Walls*

Security in converged environments requires acknowledging connectivity while limiting its implications.

Where AI applications need data but don't need to send commands, data diodes, hardware enforcing one-way communication, provide separation while enabling analytics. The AI receives operational data, analyzes it, produces insights; it cannot directly affect operations. Human operators review recommendations and decide whether to act through separate channels.

Where AI must both receive data and influence operations, connections should be as narrow as possible. Dedicated interfaces with specific, limited functions minimize attack surface. The AI that can adjust generation setpoints shouldn't have access to protection relay configurations, even if the same network could carry both.

Zero-trust principles apply, but implementation must account for legacy OT constraints. Devices from the 1980s can't support modern authentication. The zero-trust boundary may need to wrap around legacy systems rather than extend to individual devices.

Monitoring must span domains. Traditional IT security monitoring may not recognize anomalous OT protocols. OT security monitoring may not understand AI traffic patterns. Integrated monitoring that correlates activity across convergence seams can detect attacks that exploit the boundaries between different security models.

The older systems, despite their limitations, often have the best understood behavior. Decades of operation have revealed their failure modes, their performance envelopes, their quirks. New systems, including AI-enhanced systems, bring different risks. Their behavior is less understood. Their failure modes haven't been fully mapped. In the short term, replacement may actually increase operational risk, even if it reduces risk over the long term.

If your utility moves slowly on AI adoption, you're not necessarily behind. You may be appropriately cautious given what you have to lose. The conservative bias in critical infrastructure is rational risk management in a domain where consequences are severe and immediate. AI advocates who interpret caution as mere resistance to change haven't spent enough time in control rooms watching operators manage systems that cannot be allowed to fail.

The archaeology of these systems is not an obstacle to be overcome. It is a warning to be heeded. Every layer exists because something failed and someone built a response. Every undocumented practice encodes a lesson learned at cost. Every protocol limitation reflects an assumption about the world that was once accurate and may still be.

AI convergence proposes to connect, optimize, and transform these layers simultaneously. The efficiency gains are real. So is the risk of optimizing away the defenses that decades of failure taught these systems to build. The adversaries watching this transformation understand exactly what those defenses protected, and what their removal exposes.

# Chapter 6: The Adversaries Who Already Know

Somewhere in your control systems, or those of utilities you depend on, access credentials sit dormant. Obtained three years ago through a supply chain compromise no one detected. Tested periodically: brief connections that looked like routine system behavior, authentication checks that raised no alerts.

The adversary holding these credentials has mapped the network. They understand the SCADA systems, the protection schemes, the interdependencies between substations. They've identified which systems would need to fail simultaneously to cause cascading outages, which safety mechanisms would need disabling first, which operator responses would need delaying.

They haven't acted. The credentials are an option, not a plan. They'll be used if the geopolitical situation warrants, or sit dormant for another decade, waiting for a crisis that may never come.

This is what a nation-state threat looks like. Not attacks. Preparation. They're not breaking in. They're already inside, waiting.

*What Sophisticated Adversaries Actually Do*

On December 23, 2015, operators at three Ukrainian power distribution companies watched their systems behave impossibly.

Cursors moved across screens without human input. Breakers opened in substations across the country. When operators tried to regain control, they found themselves locked out: passwords changed, remote access disabled. The attackers had spent months inside these networks, learning systems, testing capabilities, positioning for the moment they chose to act.

The attack cut power to 230,000 customers. Recovery required operators to manually restore systems designed for remote operation, driving to substations in winter darkness to flip switches by hand.

The attackers demonstrated capabilities extending far beyond what the incident revealed. They had achieved access to systems they chose not to disrupt. They maintained a presence in networks they would return to for a second attack using Industroyer, which was designed to speak the protocols industrial control systems trust. The 2016 attack didn't need human interfaces. It manipulated grid equipment directly.

This is the pattern of sophisticated nation-state operations: demonstrate, withdraw, retain access. The goal isn't immediate destruction. It's positioning for conflicts that haven't yet begun.

*The Powers and What They Want*

Russian operations have demonstrated the most sophisticated attacks on critical infrastructure to date. The Ukrainian grid attacks required deep understanding of operational technology, custom malware development, and coordination across multiple stages. Russian actors have achieved access to American grid infrastructure that U.S. intelligence assessments describe as sufficient for future attacks.

Chinese operations pursue different objectives through different methods: compromising utilities, transportation systems, and communications infrastructure for reconnaissance and access maintenance rather than disruption. The goal: positioning for potential future conflict rather than current operational effects.

The patience behind that access is measured in years. Defenders find some intrusions, but methodologies designed for long-term stealth suggest discovered incidents represent a fraction of actual access. The intelligence value of sustained, undetected access is immense. And it grows as AI systems aggregate operational data that was previously fragmented across isolated systems.

Iran has demonstrated willingness to conduct destructive attacks, though technical capabilities remain below Russia and China. Iranian operations against U.S. infrastructure have generally been probing rather than penetrating, but capabilities continue to develop.

North Korea focuses primarily on financial objectives: cryptocurrency theft, bank fraud, ransomware. But it has demonstrated willingness to conduct destructive operations when politically motivated. The interconnected nature of AI-converged systems means even financially motivated attacks could produce operational disruption, as Colonial Pipeline demonstrated when ransomware on business systems shut down fuel delivery across the Eastern seaboard.

*Why AI Makes Everything Worse*

AI convergence creates opportunities these adversaries understand better than most defenders.

*Centralized targets.* AI systems synthesizing data across previously isolated systems create single points of compromise. An adversary who compromises an AI platform gains influence across every system the platform touches. One key, every door.

*Patient poisoning.* Nation-states can afford long-term operations. An adversary who can influence training data for a grid optimization AI might create subtle biases that don't manifest until crisis conditions, exactly when correct AI behavior matters most.

*Supply chain leverage.* AI systems introduce new software components, libraries, and services into infrastructure environments. Supply chain compromises targeting AI frameworks or cloud platforms could provide access to utilities deploying those components. The SolarWinds model applied to AI infrastructure.

*Intelligence acceleration.* AI systems aggregate information that previously existed in fragmented form. An adversary with access to AI analytics gains intelligence about operations, vulnerabilities, and patterns that would have required far more extensive reconnaissance from distributed systems.

AI convergence doesn't just create new vulnerabilities. It creates the concentrated, high-value targets that justify the resources nation-states invest.

*The Asymmetry You Cannot Close*

Intelligence agencies can dedicate teams of specialists to understanding a single target's systems. They can develop zero-day exploits for specific industrial control components. They can maintain a persistent presence for years while gathering intelligence for operations they may never execute. They can coordinate cyber operations with diplomatic, economic, and military activities.

Your security team cannot match these resources. You must defend against all potential attack vectors. The adversary needs to find only one.

This asymmetry drives toward collective defense. Individual utilities cannot defend against nation-state adversaries alone. Information sharing about threats, vulnerabilities, and incidents becomes essential. Government partnerships that bring intelligence capabilities become necessary complements to private security.

AI convergence compounds the asymmetry while potentially helping address it. The same AI capabilities that create new attack surfaces could enhance defensive monitoring and response, but only if defenders deploy AI security capabilities effectively while adversaries target those capabilities.

*The Patience That Terrifies*

The most concerning aspect of nation-state threats isn't their capability. It's their timeline.

The access Russia and China have obtained may sit dormant for years. The intelligence they collect may inform planning for contingencies that never occur. The capabilities they develop may never be used, or used decisively in some future crisis current planning cannot anticipate.

The credentials obtained three years ago are still valid. The network maps are still accurate, updated through connections too brief to trigger alerts. The attack plans exist in folders that may never be opened or may be opened tomorrow.

The adversary who has spent years positioning doesn't telegraph intentions. They attack when the moment maximizes strategic value: during the next international crisis, during a natural disaster when infrastructure is already stressed, or never.

AI systems being deployed today will still be operational during crises that haven't emerged. The adversaries mapping those systems think in those timescales. They are identifying how AI convergence changes the attack surface, what new pathways it creates, how centralized architectures could be exploited.

They understand the systems being built. You must understand them as well, because adversary exploitation and AI malfunction produce identical operational consequences, often indistinguishable in the moment that matters.

## Chapter 7: The Loaded Weapons

*14:47:22 PST.* A fire erupts at a Pacific Gas & Electric substation near 8th and Mission Streets in San Francisco. Protective relays isolate the affected equipment. The cascade begins immediately: 130,000 customers lose power within minutes as the fault propagates through the distribution network. Traffic signals across a third of the city go dark.

*14:52:08 PST.* Waymo's fleet management system begins receiving anomalous signals from approximately 800 robotaxis operating in San Francisco. The vehicles' autonomous systems are programmed to treat non-functional traffic signals as four-way stops. In isolation, that is a reasonable protocol. But the scale of the outage triggers something the system wasn't designed for: a concentrated spike in confirmation requests as vehicles across the city simultaneously ask the remote operations center to verify their planned actions.

*15:04:33 PST.* Videos begin appearing on social media showing Waymo vehicles stopped in intersections, hazard lights blinking, lines of human-driven cars trapped behind them. The remote operations team, designed to handle scattered edge cases, cannot process the surge of simultaneous requests. Vehicles that should have treated darkened signals as four-way stops freeze, waiting for confirmations that cannot come fast enough.

*15:31:00 PST.* City officials report that stalled robotaxis are blocking arterial roads and impeding emergency vehicles attempting to reach the substation fire. Mayor Daniel Lurie contacts Waymo's CEO directly. The company had "proactively" suspended new ride requests but had not recalled vehicles already on the street.

*19:07:00 PST.* Waymo announces service suspension. But by this point, the question has shifted. What happens when 800 vehicles freeze simultaneously was manageable, if chaotic. What happens when 8,000 freeze, or 80,000 across multiple cities during a coordinated infrastructure attack, remains unanswered.

*"We designed for the scenario we could imagine, a few signals out, scattered across the city. We didn't design for a third of the city going dark at once. The system did exactly what we told it to do. We just didn't tell it what to do in that situation."*

— Autonomous vehicle operations engineer, speaking on background

*The Pattern That Repeats*

The December 2025 incident merits attention not because robotaxis are critical infrastructure (they aren't, yet) but because they illustrate the pattern across every AI-integrated system in this sector.

Power outages affect cellular networks, which affect cloud connectivity, which affect systems designed with always-on connectivity as baseline. A fire at a single substation creates effects propagating through digital systems designed to optimize for conditions that no longer obtain.

The Waymo vehicles traversed over 7,000 darkened signals that day. But the instances where they froze, at the intersections where traffic already converged, during the conditions when human drivers most needed predictability, revealed the gap between system capability and systemic resilience.

These dependency patterns exist everywhere AI touches physical infrastructure. When the physical systems that digital systems depend on fail, those digital systems fail in ways their designers often didn't anticipate, taking the physical infrastructure they were designed to optimize down with them.

*"I tell my team: every AI system we deploy is a system that can fail. And the day it fails will be the worst possible day. A storm, a surge, an attack, that's when it fails. So we build for that day. We train for that day. And we pray we're ready when that day comes."*

— Regional Transmission Organization operations director

*How AI Systems Fail Differently*

AI systems fail in ways traditional components don't.

They hallucinate. An AI advising on generation dispatch might recommend actions that appear reasonable but reflect patterns that don't exist in the data. Unlike traditional systems, which produce obvious errors such as null values or out-of-range readings, hallucinated outputs look normal.

They drift. Models trained on historical data perform poorly when current conditions diverge from training. A model trained on normal operating data gives inappropriate recommendations during unusual events, the moments when correct recommendations matter most.

They can be manipulated. Prompt injection, data poisoning, adversarial inputs: an attacker who can influence AI recommendations might manipulate grid operations, water treatment, or transportation systems. Sophisticated attackers design manipulations that evade detection.

They require connectivity. AI systems require data sources, compute resources, and cloud services. When connectivity fails, the AI fails. Critical infrastructure must continue operating through connectivity outages: either local AI capability that functions independently or graceful fallback to non-AI operations.

*The Grid's New Minds*

The load forecasting model has been running for eighteen months. It predicts electricity demand with accuracy that exceeds human forecasters by a consistent margin. Dispatch decisions that once required experienced operators now flow through the model's recommendations. The utility saves millions annually on generation costs.

The model also learned patterns no one examined closely. Subtle correlations between sensor readings and upcoming failures. Relationships between weather forecasts and actual conditions that reflect the quirks of specific forecasting services. Connections between economic data releases and industrial load that encode timing assumptions about when factories respond to market signals.

An adversary who understands these learned patterns can exploit them. Not by attacking the model directly, but by feeding it inputs that trigger the patterns in harmful ways. Weather data that looks plausible but causes the model to systematically under-predict demand. Sensor readings that mask equipment stress. Economic indicators timed to create forecast errors during peak load conditions.

The attack doesn't look like an attack. It looks like the model performs slightly worse than usual, during conditions when slight errors compound into cascading failures.

Renewable integration models predict solar and wind output so utilities can balance variable generation with dispatchable resources. Under-predict wind generation and utilities dispatch unnecessary fossil fuel plants: economic waste. Over-predict and the grid comes up short when wind doesn't materialize. Either error cascades into instability. An attacker who can influence renewable forecasts doesn't need to compromise turbines directly. They compromise the model that tells operators what the turbines will produce.

Predictive maintenance models identify equipment at elevated failure risk before visible problems emerge. False negatives mean equipment fails without warning. False positives mean unnecessary maintenance: equipment taken offline when it could have remained in service. An adversary who can manipulate maintenance recommendations forces utilities to choose between unplanned outages and operational waste. The choice itself is the damage.

Grid optimization models handle decisions too complex for human computation: which generators to dispatch, how to route power flows, when to switch configurations. Thousands of variables, thousands of constraints, solutions that emerge from mathematical optimization rather than engineering intuition.

The security risk is severe because optimization recommendations affect physical operations. An AI that recommends dispatch changes overloading transmission lines, or switching operations that create unstable configurations, causes cascading failures. Human oversight is essential but becomes challenging as AI handles decisions faster than humans can review them.

The model that optimizes efficiently also optimizes vulnerabilities. The same capability that finds non-obvious solutions for efficiency can find non-obvious pathways to failure, if the model learns from data that teaches it wrong.

*The Chemistry That Thinks*

Water treatment operates at the intersection of chemistry and computation. AI optimizes chemical dosing, filtration rates, and treatment parameters, and it does so faster than manual processes can respond.

The security risk is a direct public health threat.

Treatment chemicals beneficial at proper concentrations become harmful at excessive levels. Sodium hydroxide adjusts pH at 100 parts per million. At 11,100 parts per million, it's poison. In February 2021, someone at the Oldsmar water treatment plant in Florida attempted that change remotely. An operator watching the screen saw the cursor move without his input and reversed the change within seconds. An AI controlling dosing could make it automatically.

The AI doesn't need to be compromised dramatically. Gradual adjustments, each within normal operating parameters, accumulating toward dangerous concentrations. The AI is doing its job, adjusting dosing based on sensor readings. The sensor data has been subtly corrupted. The optimization converges toward harm.

Leak detection models analyze pressure, flow, and acoustic sensor data to find distribution system leaks. Manipulation masks actual leaks, letting water loss, potential contamination, and infrastructure degradation compound until pipes fail catastrophically. Or it generates false leak indications that send crews to excavate functioning infrastructure, draining budgets and eroding trust.

Neither attack is dramatic. Both degrade the system's ability to maintain the infrastructure that delivers safe water to millions.

The water sector's relative obscurity in cybersecurity discussions belies its criticality. Every hospital, every school, every home depends on water treatment functioning correctly. The AI that optimizes treatment across a municipal system creates efficiency manual operation cannot match while adding centralized vulnerability manual operation never had. The manipulation that an alert operator caught in seconds at Oldsmar might take days to detect when it appears as normal AI optimization, each adjustment individually reasonable, the cumulative effect emerging gradually.

*The Networks That Move*

Traffic management AI optimizes signal timing, ramp metering, and incident response. Corrupt the inputs, and you get the opposite: congestion instead of flow, emergency vehicles trapped behind walls of stopped traffic, highways backing up during evacuation. The AI isn't malfunctioning. It's optimizing for manipulated data.

The attack might be targeted: signals around a specific location timed to delay response to an incident happening there. Or systemic: citywide disruption that overwhelms traffic management and creates gridlock that takes hours to clear. The December 2025 Waymo incident demonstrated what happens when a third of one city's signals go dark. A coordinated attack on traffic management AI across multiple cities during a crisis, whether a natural disaster or a military confrontation, could paralyze emergency response at the moment it matters most.

Pipeline operations use AI for integrity monitoring, maintenance prediction, flow optimization. Natural gas and petroleum pipelines, the arteries that deliver fuel, increasingly incorporate AI analytics for anomaly detection and operational efficiency. Colonial Pipeline showed what pipeline disruption produces even when operational technology wasn't directly compromised. AI systems that bridge IT and OT create additional pathways for disruption while potentially improving detection. The integration that lets AI spot anomalies also lets adversaries manipulate which anomalies it sees.

Rail operations demand the highest verification for any AI integration. An AI error that causes a train collision produces consequences far exceeding any efficiency gain. This creates appropriate caution. But it also means that security for deployed AI systems must be resilient.

The systems that move people and goods are becoming systems that think. What they think depends on what they learn. What they learn depends on data that can be corrupted, models that can drift, inputs that can be manipulated.

Every application is a loaded weapon. The question is who controls the trigger. The regulatory frameworks that should answer that question were written before the weapon existed. They govern the infrastructure. They do not govern the AI that increasingly controls it.

# Chapter 8: The Auditor's Silence

The auditor reviews your AI deployment documentation. She's been auditing NERC CIP compliance for fifteen years. She knows every standard, every requirement, every interpretation that's survived regional scrutiny. She doesn't know what questions to ask about the load forecasting model.

"Walk me through the access controls," she says.

The engineer explains: the model was trained on historical load data, weather feeds, and economic indicators. It runs on a cloud platform with role-based access. Authorized users can view predictions. A smaller group can adjust model parameters. An even smaller group can approve retraining.

*"And the model itself, who has access to what it knows?"*

The engineer pauses. The model doesn't "know" things the way a database stores records. It learned patterns from five years of data, including operational information that would require elevated privileges to access directly. Anyone who can query the model can ask questions that might reveal those patterns.

The access controls govern who can interact with the model. They don't govern what the model learned. The role-based permissions that NERC CIP requires don't map onto AI that synthesizes information in ways the standards never contemplated.

The auditor makes a note. She'll document what she can. The standard doesn't have a checkbox for this.

*The Grid's Framework Gap*

NERC CIP is prescriptive: it specifies required controls rather than merely requiring "adequate" security. Access management, security management, personnel training, electronic security perimeters, physical security, incident reporting, recovery planning. Each standard includes specific requirements that covered entities must implement and document.

This precision creates clarity about compliance. It also creates precision about what compliance doesn't cover.

System categorization requirements apply to "Bulk Electric System Cyber Systems" based on their impact on grid reliability. AI systems that influence grid operations may or may not fall under CIP requirements depending on implementation and function. The categorization guidance wasn't written with AI in mind.

Is a load forecasting model that influences dispatch decisions a Bulk Electric System Cyber System? What about an AI that optimizes renewable integration? What about a predictive maintenance system that determines which equipment gets taken offline?

The answers depend on interpretations that different auditors may evaluate differently. You must document your reasoning and be prepared to defend it, knowing that enforcement actions could retroactively clarify requirements you interpreted incorrectly.

Change management requirements face particular tension with AI. CIP requires documenting and testing changes to covered systems. AI models that continuously learn and update present a problem: each model update is technically a change. Treating every update as a formal change management event would make machine learning operationally impractical. Not treating them as changes may violate standards that assume systems don't modify themselves.

Audit trail requirements don't map to AI behavior. CIP requires logging electronic access. What constitutes an auditable event when an AI continuously processes data and generates outputs? The model doesn't "access" data the way a user queries a database. It learned from that data months ago, and now it produces outputs that reflect what it learned. The access happened during training. The consequences manifest during inference. The standards assume a temporal relationship between access and output that AI dissolves.

*Water's Permissive Uncertainty*

The water sector operates under less prescriptive requirements than electric utilities. That looseness creates different problems.

America's Water Infrastructure Act requires community water systems serving more than 3,300 people to conduct risk assessments and develop emergency response plans. It doesn't mandate specific cybersecurity controls. Water utilities deploying AI must determine what security is appropriate for their specific systems and risk profiles, without prescriptive standards defining adequacy.

The Environmental Protection Agency (EPA) provides guidance. The Water Information Sharing and Analysis Center offers support. These resources inform but don't mandate.

The Oldsmar incident demonstrated what inadequate water sector cybersecurity permits. In February 2021, someone remotely accessed a Florida treatment plant's control system through remote desktop software that should have been removed and briefly increased sodium hydroxide to dangerous levels. An operator caught and reversed the change within seconds. Subsequent investigation disputed whether this was a cyberattack at all. The former city manager described it as employee error, and the FBI investigation reportedly reached a similar conclusion. The distinction matters for attribution. It does not matter for the vulnerability it revealed: a treatment plant's chemical dosing was remotely adjustable, on systems running an unsupported operating system with shared passwords, without controls sufficient to prevent unauthorized changes.

Whether the cursor was moved by an adversary or an employee, the system permitted it. An AI optimizing chemical dosing across an entire treatment system creates the centralized target that Oldsmar's manual systems weren't. The efficiency gain is real. The regulatory framework that would require securing that gain barely exists.

*Transportation's Reactive Sprint*

The Colonial Pipeline attack in May 2021 triggered regulatory response at a pace the sector hadn't seen. DarkSide ransomware entered through a legacy VPN account, encrypted business systems, and led Colonial to shut down the pipeline that supplies 45 percent of the East Coast's fuel for six days. Not because attackers controlled operations, but because the company couldn't confirm attackers didn't.

Within months, TSA issued security directives requiring pipeline operators to implement network segmentation, access controls, continuous monitoring, and incident reporting. The directives were developed quickly, addressing the attack that had already occurred rather than anticipating attacks that hadn't.

Rail transportation faces similar directives. Aviation maintains its own requirements through Federal Aviation Administration (FAA) regulations. Each framework carries its own assumptions about system behavior. AI systems in transportation face compliance challenges parallel to the electric sector: continuous monitoring requirements that may conflict with AI data processing patterns, network segmentation that may conflict with AI connectivity needs.

The directives continue evolving. By the time a requirement stabilizes, the AI systems it's meant to govern have already evolved.

*The Guidance That Arrives Too Late*

The EU AI Act classifies AI systems by risk level. "High-risk" categories include AI used in critical infrastructure. High-risk systems face requirements for conformity assessments, human oversight, and documentation that go beyond traditional cybersecurity.

NIST's AI Risk Management Framework provides voluntary guidance that may eventually inform mandatory requirements. "Eventually" is doing significant work. "Voluntary" means organizations deploying AI now operate without certainty about what "compliant" will eventually mean.

Executive orders address AI in broad strokes. Agency guidance fills gaps with interpretations. Sector-specific agencies develop their own approaches, creating a patchwork that organizations must navigate without clear maps.

If you engage constructively with regulators, helping develop workable AI security standards rather than waiting, you'll shape frameworks that serve security rather than creating compliance overhead. If you wait, you may find yourself subject to requirements developed by people who never operated the systems being regulated.

*Vendors Before Standards*

Into every regulatory vacuum, vendors rush.

The gap between what NERC CIP covers and what AI deployment demands is not invisible to the market. It is an opportunity. Before regulators have determined what AI security in critical infrastructure requires, vendors are already selling it, or selling what they claim it to be.

The pattern is familiar from *The AI Convergence Trap* analysis of the AI Security-Commercial Complex, but in critical infrastructure it takes sector-specific forms. The OT security vendor that has monitored SCADA traffic for a decade rebrands its protocol analyzer as "AI-aware OT monitoring." The capability is real. The tool still detects anomalous Modbus and DNP3 traffic. What it does not do is detect adversarial inputs crafted to manipulate AI load forecasting models, identify model drift in predictive maintenance systems, or recognize when an AI's optimization is converging toward harm because its training data has been subtly poisoned. The rebranding creates the impression of coverage. The coverage does not exist.

New entrants arrive with AI-native security claims. They promise anomaly detection for AI systems operating in OT environments: monitoring model behavior, flagging inference anomalies, detecting data poisoning in sensor feeds. Some of these capabilities are genuine and valuable. Some are prototypes marketed as products, validated against simulated attacks that bear little resemblance to the patient, operationally aware adversaries documented in Chapter 6. You may lack the expertise to distinguish one from the other. The vendor's demonstration looked convincing. The competitor already bought it. The NERC CIP auditor has no framework to evaluate whether it works.

Compliance consulting compounds the dynamic. Firms that have guided utilities through NERC CIP audits for years now offer "AI governance for critical infrastructure" services. The consultants understand the regulatory landscape intimately. They may not understand machine learning at all. The deliverable is a governance framework that maps AI deployment to existing CIP requirements. The mapping produces documentation that satisfies auditors while leaving the actual AI-specific risks unaddressed. You pass the audit. The vulnerability persists.

The test is operational, not documentary. Does the monitoring tool detect the kind of attack described in Chapter 5: corrupted weather data producing systematic forecast errors that look like normal optimization? Does the governance framework address the model lifecycle questions Chapter 8 identified, where continuous learning defies change management and audit trails dissolve into inference? Does the vendor's detection capability function at the speed the grid operates, against adversaries who understand OT environments as well as the defenders do?

If the answer requires a sales presentation rather than an adversarial test, the utility has purchased reassurance. The grid does not run on reassurance. It runs on electrons and expertise, and one of those is getting harder to find.

*What Standards Already Missed*

The incidents documented throughout this section share a common feature: every one occurred within existing regulatory frameworks.

The Ukrainian grid attacks of 2015 and 2016 demonstrated what months of patient reconnaissance and deep operational understanding enable: cursors moving without input, breakers opening across the country, operators locked out of their own systems. The attackers returned a year later with protocol-native malware that didn't need human interfaces at all. These attacks targeted infrastructure governed by national security frameworks.

The frameworks didn't prevent the attacks. Manual recovery capability, a Soviet-era inheritance, is what preserved the grid.

Colonial Pipeline operated under TSA oversight when DarkSide ransomware entered through a credential that should have been decommissioned. The pipeline shut down for six days not because attackers controlled it but because existing security couldn't confirm they didn't. The $4.4 million ransom, much of it later recovered, was trivial compared to the economic damage of fuel shortages across the Eastern United States. The regulatory response arrived afterward, addressing the attack that had already happened.

Winter Storm Uri revealed what AI systems trained on historical data would inherit: the assumption that past conditions adequately represent future ones. Texas planning assumed the historical range of winter conditions was sufficient. An AI trained on the same history would have learned the same assumption. The events when correct AI behavior matters most are the events least represented in training data.

AI systems must either recognize when they're encountering conditions outside their training and disengage, or they must be trained on scenarios that include extreme events, scenarios that, by definition, have limited historical data. Neither option is simple. Both are necessary. The model that performs brilliantly during normal operations and catastrophically during emergencies is worse than no model at all. Operators who have learned to trust its recommendations will follow them into failure.

*The Uncertainty That Compounds*

Every framework examined here shares a common characteristic: it was written for systems that behave predictably, that store information in defined locations, that change through documented processes, that fail in observable ways.

AI violates these assumptions systematically.

The utility that deploys AI under NERC CIP coverage must interpret requirements for situations the standards didn't contemplate. The water system that adds AI to treatment operations must determine adequacy without prescriptive guidance to benchmark against. The pipeline operator that integrates AI for leak detection must reconcile machine learning behavior with directives written for traditional systems.

Compliance uncertainty compounds operational uncertainty. You don't just face technical questions about how to deploy AI securely. You face regulatory questions about whether your security choices will survive enforcement actions that may arrive years after deployment.

Prompt injection attacks don't appear in NERC CIP standards. Model poisoning isn't addressed in TSA directives. Adversarial manipulation isn't contemplated in EPA guidance.

The threats exist now. The frameworks that might address them are still being drafted by regulators who may not fully understand the systems they're regulating, on the basis of incidents that haven't yet forced clarity.

The standards don't speak AI. And AI isn't waiting for them to learn the language. Which leaves you where this section began: with systems that cannot fail, adversaries who have already mapped them, AI that fails differently than anything before, and frameworks that don't address the intersection. The question is no longer what might go wrong. It's what survival requires.

# Chapter 9: The Operator Who Noticed

Two utilities deployed AI load forecasting the same year. Both achieved the efficiency gains vendors promised. Both reduced generation costs. Both passed their initial security assessments.

When the coordinated attack came, corrupted weather data designed to produce systematic forecast errors during a summer heat wave, the outcomes diverged.

The first utility's AI had been integrated with operational authority. Its forecasts flowed directly to dispatch systems. Operators monitored dashboards but rarely overrode recommendations that had proven accurate for three years. When the corrupted forecasts caused under-generation during peak demand, the cascade began before anyone recognized what was happening. Rolling blackouts became sustained outages.

The second utility's AI operated in advisory mode. Its forecasts appeared alongside traditional methods. Operators compared outputs, investigated discrepancies, made decisions that incorporated AI recommendations but didn't depend on them entirely. When the same corrupted data produced the same forecast errors, an operator noticed the AI diverging from other indicators. She questioned the discrepancy. The investigation revealed the compromise before dispatch decisions were affected.

Same AI capability. Same attack. Different architectures. Different outcomes. Which one are you?

Resilient AI integration builds on a single assumption: adversaries will attempt to compromise it, and some attempts will succeed. Organizations that design for this assumption build architectures with depth. Organizations that assume prevention will suffice learn otherwise only when it's too late to recover.

Every AI component operates under suspicion. Outputs are verified before they affect operations. Recommendations require review before implementation. Access is limited to what functions require. That access is monitored for anomalies.

The trust placed in AI systems determines the consequences when that trust is misplaced. An AI with limited advisory authority, compromised, produces incorrect recommendations that humans can evaluate and reject. An AI with direct operational authority, compromised, produces consequences that manifest before evaluation is possible.

The difference between advisory and operational authority isn't bureaucratic formality. It's the distance between recoverable incident and cascading failure.

AI systems that behave unexpectedly may be compromised, drifting, or encountering conditions outside their training. Monitoring for behavioral anomalies provides early warning before problems manifest as operational failures. Even when each recommendation individually seems plausible, the model that begins recommending unusual dispatch patterns deserves investigation.

The patterns that indicate compromise are subtle. Performance degradation that appears random. Confidence scores that shift slightly. Output distributions that change gradually. Catching these patterns requires monitoring designed for AI-specific behaviors, not traditional system alerts.

Every AI-assisted function requires a non-AI alternative. The alternative will be less efficient. It must exist anyway. When AI fails, operations must continue. The utility that can revert to human-directed dispatch survives AI compromise. The utility that has eliminated manual capability because AI made it unnecessary discovers its necessity during the incident that proves otherwise.

Preserving alternatives requires intentional effort. Regular training on manual procedures. Exercises that simulate AI failure. Operational practices that maintain human situational awareness even when AI handles routine decisions. The skills atrophy if unused. The alternative must remain exercised.

Every AI integration should have documented fallback procedures: how failure is detected, who is notified, what manual procedures activate, what capability is available during degraded operations. Procedures that exist but haven't been exercised may not work when needed. The documentation is worthless if it describes processes no one has practiced. The exercise is worthless if it tests idealized conditions rather than the chaotic reality of an actual incident.

AI should operate at different levels of authority depending on consequence. For routine optimization within normal operating ranges, minimal human oversight. For significant operational changes, human confirmation is required. For safety-critical functions, AI provides information and analysis but not direct authority.

This tiering allows AI to provide value while limiting consequences of failure. An AI that can optimize routine operations but cannot override protection systems provides benefits without creating catastrophic failure potential.

AI systems should automatically disengage under conditions where their reliability degrades. When input data becomes unreliable, when connectivity is intermittent, when operating conditions diverge from training data: the AI should recognize these conditions and remove itself from operational loops. This requires AI that can assess its own confidence, which current systems can do only in limited form. It also requires operational procedures that transition from AI-assisted to human-directed operation when disengagement occurs.

*The People Who Make It Work*

Technical architecture alone is insufficient. The most sophisticated monitoring is useless if no one is watching. The most detailed procedures are useless if no one has practiced them.

AI deployment in critical infrastructure requires collaboration across traditionally separate functions. Operations understands what the systems do. IT understands how the networks connect. Security understands how adversaries attack. Compliance understands what regulations require. Executive leadership controls resources and accepts risk.

Governance that excludes any of these perspectives produces blind spots. The security team that doesn't understand operations will protect the wrong things. The operations team that doesn't understand security will create vulnerabilities through efficiency optimization. The executives who don't understand either will approve initiatives they can't evaluate.

The organizations that succeed build internal expertise bridging OT, IT, and AI domains. They hire specialists where they can find them, a scarce population. They develop existing staff through training that takes years. They partner with external resources for capabilities they can't build internally.

But they never outsource understanding entirely. When incidents occur, organizations must comprehend their own systems well enough to respond effectively. Vendor relationships that create dependency without building capability leave organizations unable to evaluate what vendors tell them.

Incident response capability must include AI-specific procedures. How do you detect that an AI system has been compromised rather than malfunctioning? How do you contain AI-driven manipulation that appears as normal optimization? How do you restore correct AI operation, or revert to non-AI alternatives, under crisis conditions?

Traditional incident response playbooks don't address these scenarios. Organizations that haven't developed AI-specific procedures discover the gap during incidents too dynamic to figure out in real time.

No organization defends alone against nation-state adversaries with patience measured in years and resources measured in dedicated teams. Information sharing about threats, vulnerabilities, and incidents provides intelligence that individual organizations cannot develop independently. Participation in sector Information Sharing and Analysis Center (ISAC)s, government partnerships, and vendor information sharing isn't optional for organizations facing sophisticated threats. It's infrastructure for survival. The utility that learns from another utility's compromise is better positioned than one that encounters the same attack without warning. The intelligence that individual organizations cannot develop independently becomes available through collective effort, even as the adversaries targeting these systems share tools, techniques, and access across national boundaries.

*The Culture That Catches Failure*

Operators steeped in safety culture bring healthy skepticism to AI recommendations. They don't blindly trust outputs because the computer says so. They question anomalies, verify unexpected recommendations, maintain situational awareness independent of what AI systems report.

This cultural foundation shouldn't be undermined by AI integration.

AI systems that present recommendations without explanation, that discourage questioning, that operate opaquely conflict with safety culture principles. Effective AI integration must complement safety culture rather than subvert it. The practical implication is that AI in critical infrastructure must be more transparent than AI in other contexts. Operators need to understand why AI recommends what it recommends, not in full mathematical detail but in operational terms that connect to their expertise and intuition.

Black-box AI that produces outputs without explanation may be acceptable for consumer applications. It's inappropriate for systems where operators must decide whether to trust AI recommendations for safety-critical functions.

*The Path That Doesn't End*

AI integration in critical infrastructure is not a project with a completion date. It's an ongoing process that evolves as AI capabilities mature, threats develop, and regulatory frameworks emerge. If you approach it as one-time implementation, you'll find yourself behind, deploying last year's defenses against this year's attacks.

To succeed, you build adaptive capability: governance structures to make ongoing decisions, technical expertise to understand evolving systems, monitoring to detect emerging problems, resilience to recover when problems occur. You treat AI integration as strategic capability requiring sustained investment, not technology deployment requiring only initial implementation.

They also maintain appropriate humility. AI systems will surprise us: with capabilities we didn't anticipate, with failures we didn't expect, with vulnerabilities we didn't imagine. The appropriate response to this uncertainty is not paralysis but preparation: building organizations that can adapt to whatever emerges rather than betting everything on predictions that may prove wrong. The organizations that thrive will be those that treat uncertainty not as a temporary condition to be eliminated but as a permanent condition to be managed.

The Ukrainian grid survived its attacks because operators could drive to substations and close breakers manually, a capability Soviet-era practice had preserved. Colonial survived its ransomware because it could, eventually, restart operations, even if the shutdown caused enormous damage in the interim. Oldsmar survived its incident because an operator was watching and caught what automated monitoring missed. Texas survived Uri because the grid, though damaged, didn't collapse entirely, and because temperatures eventually rose.

Each survival came with cost. Each revealed vulnerabilities that AI convergence expands.

The attacks that target AI systems directly haven't yet produced catastrophic infrastructure failures. That absence isn't reassurance. The adversaries who mapped Ukrainian utilities for months before striking are mapping AI systems now. The uncertainties that drove Colonial's shutdown intensify as AI creates more bridges between compromisable IT and consequential OT. The manual detection that saved Oldsmar becomes harder as AI handles more decisions automatically. The historical assumptions that failed Texas become more dangerous as AI learns from the same inadequate history.

The incidents documented here are previews. The consequences they suggest are coming.

The pattern across every incident is the same. Critical infrastructure security is not a one-time perimeter defense. It is continuous risk management. The biggest failures come from assumptions that the environment is closed, simple, or already covered by existing tools and policies. The air gap that Stuxnet crossed. The Purdue hierarchy that AI dissolved. The NERC CIP standards that assumed deterministic systems. Each failure traced back to an assumption that went unexamined until consequences made it visible.

AI convergence in critical infrastructure is inevitable. The efficiency gains are too substantial, the competitive pressures too strong, the capabilities too transformative to resist. And the consequences of getting it wrong are impossible to accept: hospitals without power, cities without water, transportation networks paralyzed.

This tension cannot be resolved through either uncritical adoption or blanket rejection. The utilities moving fastest on AI integration are often the ones with the least security expertise. The vendors promising transformation understand machine learning but not protection relays. The regulators developing frameworks are writing rules for technologies they don't fully comprehend. The gap between what AI convergence demands and what organizations can deliver is not closing. It's widening, even as deployment accelerates.

The utility that survived the coordinated attack didn't predict that specific attack. It built architecture that preserved human judgment when AI judgment failed, the architecture you need. It maintained alternatives when AI alternatives disappeared. It detected anomalies when AI anomalies emerged.

It survived not because it anticipated the threat but because it built to survive threats it couldn't anticipate.

That's what resilience means. Not prediction. Preparation.

The lights must stay on. The water must flow. The trains must run.

The transformation that offers to accomplish these functions more efficiently than ever before will accomplish them, or fail catastrophically in the attempt. The difference depends on choices being made now, by organizations that may not fully understand the systems they're deploying, against adversaries who understand those systems well.

*When You're Not the Big Grid*

The scenarios in this part describe regional grids, metropolitan water systems, statewide transportation networks. The adversaries are nation-states. The cascades affect millions. The organizations under attack have security operations centers, dedicated OT teams, regulatory compliance departments.

Most critical infrastructure operators have none of this.

The municipal water utility serving 12,000 customers runs the same SCADA architecture the majors do, an archaeology of relays, PLCs, and sensors accumulated across decades, with three full-time employees. The rural electric cooperative covers territory the size of a small state with an IT department of one. The regional transit authority operates buses and light rail with a technology team that also manages the website, the payroll system, and the security cameras.

These companies face identical convergence dynamics. Their AI exposure arrives through the same vendor platforms serving the largest utilities: the same load forecasting models, the same sensor analytics, the same predictive maintenance tools. The vulnerability surface is shared. The resources to address it are not.

The structural asymmetry is worth naming. Small utilities cannot negotiate vendor contracts. They accept standard terms or they do not participate. They cannot audit model training pipelines. They cannot staff 24/7 security monitoring. They cannot maintain parallel manual systems as backup. The Oldsmar water plant, where an operator caught the unauthorized change because he was watching the screen, had fifteen employees serving 15,000 people. That operator's presence was not a security architecture. It was a coincidence that happened to prevent a dangerous outcome.

AI convergence makes that coincidence less likely, not more. When the AI handles dosing adjustments automatically, when optimization runs continuously without an operator staring at a screen, the window for human detection narrows to the point where the word "oversight" becomes aspirational rather than descriptive.

Resource-constrained utilities have limited but real options. *The AI Convergence Trap* detailed the strategic framework: concentrate vendor relationships rather than diversifying governance attention across too many providers. Choose vendors serving large utilities, because enterprise customers negotiate the security standards smaller organizations inherit. Document what data touches AI systems, what decisions incorporate AI outputs, and what human review occurred. Maintain exit plans before dependency becomes lock-in.

For critical infrastructure specifically, three additional principles apply.

First, preserve manual capability as if lives depend on it, because they do. The Ukrainian grid survived its cyberattack because operators could drive to substations and close breakers by hand. A small utility that allows manual operational knowledge to atrophy in favor of AI optimization has eliminated its last line of defense. The manual procedures may be slower. They must remain executable.

Second, treat the regional mutual aid network as your security architecture. Small utilities cannot build detection and response capabilities alone. Information Sharing and Analysis Centers exist because individual utilities cannot maintain the threat intelligence that collective participation provides: the Electricity Information Sharing and Analysis Center (E-ISAC) for electric, WaterISAC for water. The cooperative that shares incident indicators strengthens every member. The one that operates in isolation absorbs every attack alone.

Third, know which AI decisions carry physical consequences and put human gates on those decisions specifically. A small utility cannot review every AI output. It can ensure that decisions affecting chemical dosing, voltage regulation, valve positions, and other actuations that cross the boundary from digital to physical require human confirmation. The AI can recommend. A human must execute. Imperfect, slow, expensive, that single constraint is the difference between optimization and catastrophe when the model is wrong.

The gap between what AI convergence requires and what small operators can realistically provide continues to widen. Recognizing this is not an excuse for inaction but a call for honesty about what protections are achievable, which risks must be tolerated, and who bears the weight of those choices. The consequences don't rest on a utility's balance sheet; they fall on the communities that rely on its water, power, and infrastructure to work safely, even when the AI does not.

*What This Reveals*

The grid does not answer to twelve jurisdictions, it barely answers to one. And everything else depends on it.

This is the first lesson of critical infrastructure under AI convergence: the sectors with the lightest governance bear the most consequential risks. The cascades that will darken hospitals and freeze trading floors will begin in systems where no compliance officer has mapped an AI deployment, where no model risk team has validated the training data, where no governance committee has asked what happens when the optimization is wrong. The regulatory density downstream cannot compensate for the regulatory vacuum upstream. The dominoes fall from where we are least watching toward where we are watching most, and by then, watching is all that remains.

The second lesson is temporal. Seconds. The interval between AI decision and physical consequence in these systems is measured in the time it takes a relay to close, a valve to open, a transformer to adjust. There is no eleven-minute window. There is no human review for individual decisions. There is only the architecture you built before the moment arrived: the manual capability you preserved or abandoned, the human judgment you maintained or optimized away, the override authority you protected or dissolved. When the AI is wrong about something that matters, the only question is whether you built systems that can survive being wrong. The Ukrainian grid answered that question with operators driving to substations in winter darkness. The answer your systems would give is being written now, in every deployment decision that trades resilience for efficiency.

# Part III : Healthcare

## Chapter 10: When the Diagnosis Is Wrong

In March 2023, a 52-year-old woman arrived at a teaching hospital with symptoms no one could explain. The hospital's AI analyzed her records: lab work, imaging, eighteen months of history. Its assessment: early-stage pancreatic cancer, 94% confidence. The system recommended immediate surgical consultation and staging workup.

The attending physician, pressed for time and impressed by the AI's apparent certainty, ordered the recommended workup. Over the following weeks, the patient underwent Computed Tomography (CT) scans, Magnetic Resonance Imaging (MRI) studies, endoscopic ultrasound, and eventually an exploratory laparotomy, invasive surgery to directly examine her pancreas.

The surgeon found nothing. No cancer. No tumor. The AI had hallucinated a diagnosis from patterns that, in retrospect, suggested nothing more than chronic pancreatitis.

The patient recovered from her unnecessary surgery. Her trust in the healthcare system did not. The hospital faced a malpractice claim that settled for an undisclosed amount. Somewhere in a quality improvement meeting, administrators debated whether the AI system should be decommissioned, retrained, or simply given a disclaimer telling physicians not to trust it too much.

The hallucination that corrupts a grid optimization algorithm is dangerous. The hallucination that appears in a diagnostic recommendation is personal. It happens to your patients, people who trusted the system to help them.

Critical infrastructure demonstrated what happens when AI failures affect populations: blackouts, water contamination, transportation disruptions. Healthcare shifts the frame from infrastructure serving populations to systems serving individuals. The stakes are measured in diagnoses, treatments, and lives. The consequences are experienced personally, in examination rooms and hospital beds, by patients and families who may never understand why the technology they trusted failed them.

Human clinicians typically intervene between AI output and patient outcome. A diagnostic AI that hallucinates misinforms the physician who might then make a harmful decision. This human mediation provides a buffer, but one AI convergence is eroding.

AI-guided surgical robots respond in real-time to intraoperative conditions. Automated medication dispensing systems fill prescriptions with minimal oversight. Algorithmic treatment protocols determine chemotherapy dosing. Each advancement reduces the human buffer while eliminating a layer of defense against AI errors.

The erosion is already underway. The buffer that once gave you time to catch errors, to apply clinical judgment, to notice that something didn't feel right is being thinned, visit by visit, innovation by innovation, until what remains is insufficient to catch the errors that matter most.

Consent issues arise when AI synthesizes patient information in ways no consent form contemplated. Bias implications emerge when algorithms trained on historical data perpetuate the healthcare disparities that data reflects. The irreducible need for human judgment clashes with efficiency pressures that tempt organizations to automate what should not be automated.

If your health system understands these dynamics, you are building systems that capture AI's benefits while protecting patients from its risks. If not, you are discovering consequences the way healthcare always has: through patient harm.

The scenarios throughout this part often describe large health systems: academic medical centers with Chief Medical Information Officers and AI governance committees, teaching hospitals where a skeptical pathologist can question a 94% confidence score, regional systems with resources to staff cross-functional oversight. The risks are clearest there because visibility is greatest.

Most healthcare operates differently. The critical access hospital with twenty-five beds. The independent primary care practice running on an EHR whose AI features activated by default in the last update. The community health center treating patients in twelve languages with a technology budget that covers licensing fees and nothing else. These providers face identical convergence dynamics, amplified by constraints the academic medical center does not share: the same hallucination risks, the same bias patterns, the same consent paradoxes.

Chapter 14 addresses what these dynamics mean when the resources to address them don't exist. The community hospital adopting AI through its EHR vendor inherits the same risks as the academic medical center with none of the institutional infrastructure to manage them. The risks documented here apply everywhere. The capacity to address them does not. Read with that asymmetry in mind.

*The Weight of a Single Error*

A clinical decision support system flags a patient for possible early-onset dementia. Confidence score 87%. The physician has eleven minutes before the next patient. The AI synthesized eighteen months of data points: a missed appointment, a late prescription renewal, an incorrect self-reported reading. None individually suggests cognitive decline. The AI sees a pattern.

The physician begins a conversation that cannot be un-had.

What the AI doesn't know: the missed appointment coincided with a spouse's hospitalization. The late renewal happened during the funeral. The incorrect reading came from a monitor with dying batteries. The patient is grieving, not declining.

The neuropsychological evaluation finds nothing wrong. But the two weeks of fear, the whispered family conversations, the way the patient now second-guesses every forgotten word. These are real consequences of an AI hallucination that, by every technical metric, performed exactly as designed. No adverse event report will be filed. The harm was invisible to every measurement system the hospital operates. But ask Mrs. Chen if it was real.

*Why Medical Hallucinations Kill*

Medical AI hallucinations carry false authority. A diagnostic AI trained on millions of patient records appears to possess expertise no individual physician could match. When it offers a recommendation with high confidence, it invokes the implicit authority of all that training data. Physicians, especially those early in their careers, defer to the AI's apparent expertise even when their own clinical intuition suggests something different.

The confidence score itself becomes the problem. A physician who isn't sure might say "this could be pancreatic cancer, but I'd want to rule out other possibilities first." An AI system reports "94% probability of pancreatic cancer," a number that implies precision the underlying model doesn't possess. That number comes from mathematical properties of the model's output distribution, not genuine epistemic certainty about the diagnosis.

Medical hallucinations are difficult to detect. Unlike a hallucinated contract clause verifiable against the actual contract, a hallucinated diagnosis cannot be immediately verified. The patient's actual condition must be discovered through clinical investigation that itself takes time and carries risks. The only way to definitively refute the recommendation is to complete the diagnostic workup the recommendation triggered. You won't know it was unnecessary until results come back.

The harm compounds. A misdiagnosis redirects the entire course of care. The patient treated for the wrong condition isn't being treated for the right one. Treatments for the hallucinated condition may themselves cause harm: unnecessary surgery, toxic medications, radiation exposure.

A patient told they have cancer experiences profound psychological trauma even if the diagnosis is later corrected. The weeks of believing they faced a terminal illness, the conversations with family, the arrangements made: these cannot be undone by "never mind, the AI was wrong."

The hallucinations take distinct forms. *Diagnostic hallucinations* generate false diagnoses from pattern artifacts, as when an AI trained on academic medical center data develops systematic false positives for rare conditions. *Treatment hallucinations* recommend inappropriate interventions: drug interactions unweighted, dosing that ignores organ function, contraindications overlooked.

Most insidious are *synthesis hallucinations*: the AI correctly identifies individual data points but combines them incorrectly, creating composite pictures that misrepresent the patient's clinical state. Documentation hallucinations fall here too: fabricated details enter the record and propagate indefinitely, the hallucination becoming "real" because it influences future care.

How would you have detected that the pancreatic cancer recommendation was a hallucination? The symptoms were real. The laboratory values were real. The AI had access to all the same information the physician did, yet appeared to see patterns the physician couldn't. Refuting it required the very workup the recommendation had triggered. This circularity, the AI's recommendation creating the conditions for its own apparent validation, is what makes medical hallucinations structurally different from hallucinations in other domains.

*The Defenses That Might Work*

Verification layers add checkpoints before AI recommendations reach the physician. Rule-based filters catch biologically implausible suggestions. Knowledge graphs check whether the relationships the AI found actually appear in medical literature. Second-opinion mechanisms query alternative models to identify discrepancies. These verification layers reduce the speed and efficiency that motivated AI adoption in the first place. Organizations must balance thoroughness against practical constraints of clinical workflow. Competitive pressure tends to resolve that balance in favor of speed.

Confidence calibration transforms raw model outputs into clinically meaningful uncertainty expressions. A recommendation with "94% confidence" might be better expressed as "strongly suggests, but recommend confirmatory testing," language that communicates the model's assessment without implying false precision. Calibration requires ongoing monitoring as models drift over time.

Explainability requirements demand that AI systems provide reasoning physicians can evaluate. A recommendation without explanation can't be critically assessed. When the AI shows which features drove its conclusion, physicians can evaluate whether those features actually support it. But the explanations AI systems provide are themselves generated outputs, not windows into actual mathematical processes. An AI might cite a symptom as evidence for its diagnosis even when that symptom barely influenced its output. The explanation is plausible but not necessarily accurate.

Human oversight mandates establish requirements for physician involvement in AI influenced decisions. High-stakes decisions such as cancer diagnoses, surgical recommendations, and end-of-life care should require explicit physician attestation that they have independently evaluated the AI's recommendation rather than accepting it. But the mandate must be more than checkbox compliance. Clicking "I reviewed this" while already reaching for the next chart isn't oversight. It's theater. And theater provides no protection. The workflow must make genuine review of the path of least resistance.

Mrs. Chen's case will appear in no quality report. The neuropsychological evaluation found nothing wrong. By every metric the hospital tracks, the system performed correctly. But in a house somewhere in the city, a woman who spent two weeks believing she was losing her mind now flinches whenever she forgets a word. Her daughter watches her more closely than before. The fear was never fully resolved. The AI will recommend the same pattern tomorrow. The confidence score will display the same false precision. The physician will have the same eleven minutes.

# Chapter 11: The Patient No One Sees

She paid cash for the psychiatrist. Cash—not insurance, not even a personal check that would show the practice's name. She scheduled appointments during lunch breaks, told no one at work, kept the antidepressants in an unmarked bottle. For three years, she maintained a wall between her mental health treatment and the rest of her medical record.

The hospital's AI system figured it out anyway.

It wasn't told about the psychiatrist. It never accessed those records. They didn't exist in any system it could reach. But it noticed patterns in her other care. The primary care visits scheduled at unusual intervals. The way she declined certain medications that might interact with antidepressants. The gaps in her record during times when someone managing depression might step back from routine care. The questions she asked her physician, phrased carefully but carrying the vocabulary of someone who'd discussed medication side effects before.

The AI flagged her for mental health follow-up. The recommendation appeared on her new physician's screen: "Pattern analysis suggests possible undisclosed psychiatric treatment. Consider direct inquiry regarding mental health history."

Her deliberate choice to maintain privacy was defeated not by a breach, but by synthesis. No one hacked her records. The AI figured it out.

*What Synthesis Reveals*

Prescription patterns indicate conditions patients have never disclosed: anxiety medications, HIV prophylaxis, addiction treatment. Appointment scheduling patterns reveal employment situations or relationship changes. Individually innocuous data points combine to infer sensitive information patients chose to conceal.

Genetic information amplifies these concerns. A patient's genetic data, synthesized with health history and family records, enables predictions about future conditions the patient may not want to know, let alone have documented in records employers or insurers might access. The synthesis extends to families: health information about one family member enables inferences about others. A parent's genetic condition implies probabilities about their children's genetic status. AI synthesis that considers family relationships, as good clinical AI should, uses information about people who never consented. The patient who opted into genetic testing did not opt their children into probabilistic health predictions. But the AI, operating correctly, generates those predictions anyway.

*The Paradox That Cannot Be Solved*

Here is the truth healthcare AI governance cannot escape: meaningful consent for AI synthesis may be impossible.

Patients cannot consent to inferences they cannot anticipate. No consent form can enumerate the patterns an AI might find, the conclusions it might draw. The patient signing a form today cannot know what tomorrow's AI will be capable of inferring from their data.

Yet requiring explicit consent for each new AI capability would halt healthcare AI development. No provider could deploy AI if every algorithmic improvement required returning to millions of patients for new consent. The patients who most need AI-enabled care improvements often cannot provide it: the seriously ill, the cognitively impaired, the deceased whose records still inform AI training.

This is a genuine paradox, not a problem awaiting a clever solution. You can choose paternalism: deciding for patients what AI uses are acceptable. Or you can choose paralysis and abandon AI uses that might benefit patients. What you cannot choose is an option that fully respects both patient autonomy and AI potential. That option does not exist.

*"Every consent form we write is a fiction. We ask patients to authorize uses of their data that we can't fully describe, for purposes we can't fully anticipate, by systems that will change after they sign. We call it 'informed consent' but the information is incomplete and the consent is to something we don't fully understand ourselves."*

— Privacy Officer, Regional Health System

*Living With the Paradox*

Patients should know when AI systems are analyzing their records, what types of analysis are being performed, and what kinds of inferences might be generated. This transparency won't eliminate the paradox. Patients still can't meaningfully consent to inferences they can't anticipate. But it ensures they know their information is being processed in ways traditional care didn't involve. Transparency requires accessible communication. A dense technical disclosure buried in admission paperwork doesn't constitute meaningful notice.

Opt-out mechanisms allow patients who object to synthesis to exclude their records from AI processing. This creates operational challenges, as the AI must respect exclusions without degrading performance, but provides meaningful choice for patients who want one. The challenge is that patients who most need protection may be least likely to exercise it. Patients with stigmatized conditions, marginalized populations, or limited health literacy may not understand the option or feel empowered to use it. Opt-out shifts burden to patients rather than addressing the design choices that create synthesis risks.

Inference limitations constrain what AI systems are permitted to infer. A practice might decide its AI will not generate inferences about mental health conditions, genetic risks, or other sensitive categories, even if technically possible. These limitations sacrifice capability to protect privacy. Implementing inference limitations requires technical controls, not just policy declarations. The AI must be designed to avoid certain inference types, and those constraints must be verified through testing. Announcing that the AI "doesn't do" certain things while allowing it full access to enabling data provides no protection.

The woman who paid cash for the psychiatrist will never know her privacy was compromised by inference rather than breach. The flag in her chart looks like any other recommendation. The synthesis that revealed what she chose to hide operates unseen, documented nowhere, violating nothing the law prohibits.

*The Patient the Algorithm Doesn't See*

The same AI that sees too much of some patients sees too little of others.

The algorithm identified patients who would benefit from intensive care management: chronic conditions, complex needs, high utilization likely without intervention. Resources flowed to those the model flagged.

Charlene Williams was not flagged.

Her diabetes had been poorly controlled for years. Her hypertension required medication adjustments her primary care physician didn't have time to make. Her depression, undiagnosed and untreated, kept her from following through on appointments. By every clinical measure, she was the patient who would benefit from care management.

The algorithm didn't see her. It learned to identify patients by healthcare spending, which is, in theory, a reasonable proxy for healthcare need. But Charlene, like many Black patients in America, faced barriers to care access that suppressed her spending. She couldn't take time off her hourly job. The specialists she needed didn't accept her insurance. The transportation to reach them didn't exist in her neighborhood.

Her low spending taught the algorithm she had low needs. Her actual needs remained invisible.

The Optum algorithm systematically underselected Black patients for care management; the analysis that exposed it found that fixing the racial disparity would increase Black patient enrollment from 17.7% to 46.5%. The algorithm wasn't racist in its intent. It accurately identified lower spending. It incorrectly equated lower spending with lower need.

*What the Training Data Contains*

Healthcare AI learns from the healthcare that happened. If Black patients with chest pain historically received less aggressive cardiac workups than white patients with similar presentations, and they did. An AI trained on that data learns that Black patients with chest pain are less likely to have cardiac disease. The AI isn't racist. It's accurately reflecting patterns in data. Those patterns mirror racist care disparities.

If dermatology AI trains primarily on images of light-skinned patients, it performs poorly evaluating conditions on dark-skinned patients. If speech recognition for clinical documentation trains primarily on native English speakers, it struggles with accented speech. These aren't subtle algorithmic issues. They're straightforward gaps in training data that translate to straightforward gaps in performance.

The feedback loop perpetuates itself. A diagnostic AI that underdiagnoses a condition in a certain population leads to fewer diagnoses in that population, which becomes training data suggesting the condition is less common in that population, which reinforces the underdiagnosis. The bias amplifies through each cycle.

If the AI predicts which patients will develop complications, and the complication rates in training data were influenced by differential treatment, the AI learns patterns that may not apply when treatment is equitable. It predicts that marginalized patients are more likely to have complications, because the training data reflected a world where those patients received worse care.

*Where Bias Kills*

A skin cancer detection AI achieves 95% accuracy in light-skinned patients and 70% accuracy in dark-skinned patients. The aggregate performance metrics that vendors report and purchasers evaluate show 92% overall accuracy. Excellent, by any standard. The patients whose cancers are missed at higher rates don't appear in the aggregate metrics. Their delayed diagnoses, their advanced-stage treatments, their shortened lives: these consequences hide behind a number that looks reassuring.

Risk stratification tools determine which patients receive intensive interventions. The Optum pattern of underestimating risk in populations that historically received less care could affect which patients get enrolled in disease management, which get home health visits, which get proactive outreach. Treatment recommendation systems trained on historical prescribing learn that certain populations receive different treatments. Patients with limited English proficiency received simpler regimens, perhaps because providers assumed they couldn't manage complex ones. The AI learns to recommend simpler regimens for future patients with limited English proficiency. The assumption perpetuates.

Resource allocation algorithms carry the highest stakes. Which patients get Intensive Care Unit (ICU) beds, specialist appointments, organ transplants. An algorithm that systematically disadvantages certain populations in organ matching makes life-or-death decisions based on historical patterns that should be corrected, not perpetuated.

Organizations deploying healthcare AI must evaluate performance separately across demographic groups. Overall accuracy is necessary but not sufficient. A system that works well for most patients while failing specific populations causes harm that aggregate metrics hide.

The challenge is that disaggregated analysis requires demographic data, and demographic data in healthcare is inconsistent. Race, ethnicity, and language information may be incomplete or inaccurate. Outcome monitoring by population tracks whether AI-influenced decisions lead to different outcomes for different groups. Clinician overrides, tracked by patient characteristics, reveal patterns: if clinicians consistently override recommendations for certain populations, either the AI isn't performing well for those populations or clinician biases are overriding appropriate recommendations.

The organizations doing this work are rare. The competitive pressure to deploy AI focuses on capability and efficiency, not on disaggregated performance that might reveal problems no one wants to find.

Charlene Williams received her care management enrollment two years later, after a hospitalization that could have been prevented. The algorithm has been adjusted. But the pattern it exemplified operates far beyond Optum: AI learning from historical data that encodes historical disparities now shapes diagnostic systems, treatment recommendations, and resource allocation tools across American healthcare. The patient the algorithm doesn't see remains invisible until the consequences become undeniable, and by then, the harm has already occurred.

# Chapter 12: Eleven Minutes

Dr. Okonkwo has eleven minutes.

That's the average: insurance reimbursement rates, panel size, overhead costs, all the math that determines how healthcare actually works. Eleven minutes to review the chart, greet the patient, take a history, perform an examination, consider differentials, order tests, prescribe treatments, document everything, and address whatever concern brought the patient here today.

The AI's recommendation appears on her screen. Confidence score 87%. The blue box sits there, waiting.

She could independently evaluate the recommendation. Review the eighteen months of data the AI synthesized. Consider alternative explanations for each data point. Apply her own clinical judgment to the pattern the AI identified. Decide whether the correlation suggests causation, whether the pattern indicates pathology.

That evaluation would take twenty minutes. She has eleven.

*"We tell ourselves there's always a human in control. But watch a code sometime. The AI says v-fib, we shock. The AI says asystole, we don't. We're not overseeing anything. We're following."*

— Emergency Medicine Physician, Level I Trauma Center

*When Seconds Decide*

The cardiac arrest patient has no time for oversight. The AI analyzes rhythm, displays its assessment, prompts the protocol. The code team responds in a choreography drilled until it becomes reflex: chest compressions, airway management, medication administration. If the AI misidentifies the rhythm, the wrong intervention follows. In the chaos of a code, with alarms sounding and a patient dying on the table, questioning doesn't happen.

The AI-guided surgical robot analyzes tissue characteristics in real-time, adjusting cutting paths and cauterization intensity. Human oversight of each micro-decision is impossible. The decisions happen faster than human perception. The surgeon can override, but only if they notice something wrong, and by then the AI has made thousands of additional decisions.

The ICU monitoring AI watches patients continuously, adjusting ventilator settings, titrating vasopressors, managing fluid balance. A human could review each adjustment, but doing so would require one-to-one staffing no ICU can afford.

The efficiency gain that justifies deployment is incompatible with the oversight that would ensure safety.

The standard answer, that AI should recommend and humans should decide, doesn't survive contact with clinical reality. In time-critical situations, the distinction between recommendation and decision collapses. A recommendation that must be accepted or rejected in seconds, without time for independent analysis, is functionally a decision. You become a rubber stamp, providing legal cover without actual oversight.

*The Design That Cannot Fully Compensate*

Tiered oversight requirements establish different standards for different decision types. Seconds-level decisions require only that AI recommendations be presented, with providers trained to recognize common error patterns. Minutes-level decisions require explicit provider confirmation. Hours-level decisions require documented independent analysis. Days-level decisions require multidisciplinary review. The tiers must be defined before the moment arrives. A provider under time pressure shouldn't have to decide what level of oversight is appropriate. The system should already know based on decision type and clinical context.

Pre-validated pathways reduce real-time oversight burden by front-loading human judgment. If a clinical committee has reviewed and approved an AI-guided protocol for a specific scenario, individual providers can follow that protocol without re-analyzing the AI's reasoning in each case. The oversight happened during protocol development. But pre-validated pathways assume the patient fits the pathway. Patients who present atypically, whose conditions don't match the protocol's assumptions, or whose preferences don't align with standard approach require individualized evaluation that pre-validation can't provide.

Retrospective review accepts that real-time oversight may be impossible and builds learning from after-the-fact analysis. Cases where AI recommendations were followed under time pressure get reviewed subsequently, identifying error patterns that might prompt protocol changes. Retrospective review doesn't prevent harm in individual cases. The patient harmed by an AI error under time pressure isn't helped by the subsequent review. But it can prevent systematic harm if the review identifies recurring patterns.

Override documentation creates accountability when providers choose not to follow AI recommendations. If the AI recommends one course and the provider chooses another, the decision gets documented with reasoning. The documentation requirement must not become an obstacle to appropriate overrides. If providers feel that disagreeing with the AI requires extensive justification, they follow recommendations they doubt to avoid the documentation burden. The goal is capturing reasoning for learning, not creating barriers to independent judgment.

*The Professionals Who Remain*

Maria has been a nurse for twenty-three years. She remembers when she could look at a patient and know something was wrong before any monitor alarmed. She learned to read patients like texts, accumulating pattern recognition that no textbook could teach: the color of skin, the rhythm of breathing, the subtle restlessness that preceded deterioration.

Now the AI reads them instead.

The clinical surveillance system analyzes vital signs, laboratory trends, medication interactions, documentation patterns. It catches things Maria might miss and misses things Maria would catch. The judgment she spent decades developing has become one input among many, and not always the decisive one.

This morning, the AI says nothing about the patient in 412. Vitals stable. Labs unremarkable. The algorithm sees a patient who doesn't need intervention.

Maria sees something else. A quality she can't name: the way he's holding himself, the micro-expressions when he thinks no one is watching, something in the breathing pattern the monitors don't capture. Twenty-three years of pattern recognition firing on signals too subtle for sensors.

She escalates anyway.

Dr. James Chen has been a radiologist for eighteen years. He chose the specialty because he loved the puzzle: looking at images, finding the subtle abnormality, making the diagnosis that changed the patient's trajectory. Now the AI analyzes CT scans, chest X-rays, mammograms. It flags abnormalities, suggests diagnoses, measures tumors. His role has shifted from diagnostician to quality controller. He reviews AI outputs rather than generating his own interpretations.

Today, there's nothing to review. The AI found nothing. Maria is asking him to look anyway.

"The system says he's fine," he tells her. It's not a dismissal. It's an observation. He knows what she's asking. He knows what the documentation will require if he orders imaging without algorithmic indication.

"The system doesn't know what I know," Maria says.

Dr. Chen looks at the chart. Looks at Maria. Eighteen years ago, this wouldn't have been a conversation. He would have ordered the scan based on a nurse's clinical concern. Now there are override rates to consider, efficiency metrics, the documentation burden that falls on both of them when they contradict the algorithm.

He orders the scan.

The images come back. Dr. Chen sits at his workstation, and for a moment he's not reviewing AI outputs. He's doing what he trained to do, what he loved about this specialty before the algorithms arrived. Reading the images himself. Finding the pattern.

There it is. Small, early, exactly where the AI's training data had a gap. The kind of finding that requires a human eye looking for something the system wasn't built to see.

The patient will live because Maria trusted what she knew and Dr. Chen trusted Maria. The system will never register this save. No metric captures the diagnosis the AI would have missed.

But the override, that gets documented. Maria's override rate ticks up. She's already been counseled about being an "outlier." Dr. Chen's efficiency metrics take a hit for ordering imaging without algorithmic indication. Somewhere in the quality improvement database, this case registers as a deviation from protocol, not a success of clinical judgment. Why would it register any other way? The system measures what it was built to measure.

Her expertise hasn't disappeared. It's been subordinated. His hasn't vanished. It's been reclassified as inefficiency.

They share a look in the hallway afterward. Two professionals who remember when this exchange felt different. When a nurse's concern led naturally to a physician's investigation, without metrics or documentation burden or counseling sessions about override rates. The younger staff don't understand what the work used to feel like. Maria and Dr. Chen remember, and grieve something they can't quite articulate.

Diagnostic specialties face selective pressure across the board. Radiology, pathology, and dermatology, where diagnosis depends on pattern recognition, see AI capabilities approaching or exceeding human performance in narrow domains. Specialists resist AI that threatens their discipline while recognizing it provides genuine clinical value.

The generational dynamics cut both ways. Physicians trained before AI may be appropriately skeptical, or inappropriately dismissive. Younger physicians, trained with AI from residency onward, may be appropriately integrated, or inappropriately dependent. Neither reflexive rejection nor uncritical acceptance serves patients.

Administrative workers face the highest displacement risk. These functions are amenable to automation: billing, scheduling, prior authorization, documentation transcription. The workers performing them have detailed operational knowledge without the clinical training that might protect them. They also have broad access to patient information for legitimate business purposes. Facing displacement, some become disgruntled insiders with both motive and access to cause harm. The efficiency gains from automating their work come with insider threat risks that security teams must anticipate.

*The Atrophying Safety Net*

The Boeing 737 MAX disasters happened because the humans who would have caught the problems were gone: displaced, overruled, ignored. The engineers with institutional knowledge about failure modes had been pushed out. The pilots facing automated systems they didn't understand lacked training to diagnose what was happening.

Healthcare faces analogous dynamics. The nurse who used to catch deterioration through clinical observation now monitors AI alerts. The radiologist who used to find subtle abnormalities now reviews AI-flagged findings. The pharmacist who used to catch dangerous interactions now confirms AI-generated warnings. Each transition makes sense individually. The aggregate effect is a system increasingly dependent on AI functioning correctly.

When the AI fails, the humans must take over. But the humans have been practicing AI-augmented medicine for years. Their unaugmented skills have atrophied. The institutional knowledge about how to practice without AI support lives in professionals who are retiring, who learned medicine in a different era, who aren't being replaced by new graduates with equivalent capability.

Eliminate the humans who understand the edge cases, and edge cases become catastrophes.

Maria's pattern recognition still matters, and the patient in 412 proves it. But every time she uses it, she pays a cost the system was designed to impose. The profession she entered is not the profession she practices now. Her successor, trained with AI from day one, has never developed the same pattern recognition. Never needed to. The AI was always there. And when it misses something, when it inevitably misses something, there may be no Maria left to see what it cannot.

The next time Maria sees something the algorithm doesn't, she'll have to decide again whether the documentation burden, the metrics hit, the counseling session, are worth trusting what twenty-three years taught her to see.

The last redundancy isn't a technical system. It's the human beings who remember how to practice medicine when the technical systems fail. They're still here. They won't always be.

Dr. Okonkwo looks at the blue box on her screen. Mrs. Chen's daughter sits beside her mother, unaware that a recommendation waits for action. Eleven minutes. The AI's confidence score implies it has done what she cannot do: synthesized eighteen months of data, identified patterns, reached a conclusion. The work of hours compressed into a number: 87%. She could ignore the recommendation. But last month, the system caught a cancer she might have missed. The patient is alive because she took the AI seriously. She could accept the recommendation. But the eleven minutes don't include time to explain what cognitive decline means, what the evaluation involves, what the family should expect. The conversation will run long. Her afternoon schedule will cascade. She could investigate further. Review the data points the AI identified. Look for alternative explanations. Apply the judgment she spent years developing. That investigation would take twenty minutes. She has eleven.

The patient is grieving, not declining. Dr. Okonkwo doesn't know this yet. The AI doesn't know it either.

She begins the conversation.

# Chapter 13: 3:47 AM on a Saturday

The auditor's question seems simple: "When the AI synthesizes information across the patient's record, who authorized that synthesis?"

The compliance officer pauses. The patient signed a consent for treatment. The consent authorizes use of information for treatment, payment, and healthcare operations. The AI is part of healthcare operations. Therefore the synthesis is authorized.

But the consent was signed in 2019, before the AI system existed. The patient agreed to share information with their providers. Did they agree to have an AI combine eighteen months of data points into an inference about cognitive decline? Did they agree to synthesis that reveals patterns they never consciously disclosed?

HIPAA authorizes disclosure for treatment without requiring specific consent for each disclosure. But AI synthesis isn't a disclosure in the traditional sense. The information doesn't move; it transforms. The AI doesn't access psychiatric records and share them. It infers psychiatric conditions from other records that were appropriately accessed. The violation, if it is one, isn't in the access. It's in the inference.

HIPAA doesn't clearly address inferences.

*The Rules That Don't Fit*

The category of AI that qualifies as an FDA-regulated medical device keeps expanding. A diagnostic AI submitted for approval is frozen at that moment. The FDA evaluates that version; the approval covers that version.

But an AI that learns from new data is a different system than the one approved. The model that passed regulatory review last year has been updated with this year's data. Is it still approved? The FDA has proposed frameworks for "predetermined change control plans" that would allow certain modifications without new submissions. The frameworks remain in development. Organizations deploying AI now make judgment calls about which modifications require new regulatory submissions.

The boundary between regulated medical devices and unregulated clinical decision support remains contested. The FDA won't regulate clinical decision support where the user can "independently review the basis for the recommendation." But can a physician independently review the basis for a recommendation generated by an opaque neural network? The basis exists as mathematical weights across billions of parameters. No human can review that. The carve-out assumes review is possible. For many AI systems, it isn't.

State-level regulation fragments further. California proposes regulations on automated decision systems. Colorado requires disclosures for high-risk AI. A health system operating in multiple states faces different requirements in each: requirements that may conflict, evolving at different speeds, assuming different definitions of what AI even is. State medical practice acts affect who can rely on AI recommendations. If an AI makes diagnostic recommendations, does acting on them constitute practicing medicine? Can a nurse practitioner rely on AI recommendations that exceed their scope of practice under state law?

Malpractice law creates liability exposure that varies by state. A physician who follows a reasonable AI recommendation faces liability if the recommendation was wrong. A physician who rejects a correct AI recommendation faces liability for not using available tools. The standard of care, against which malpractice claims are evaluated, is complicated when AI recommendations don't align with traditional clinical practice.

The EU AI Act classifies healthcare AI as high-risk, imposing requirements for risk management, transparency, human oversight, and accuracy that exceed U.S. requirements. The GDPR provides stronger individual data rights than HIPAA, including rights to explanation of automated decisions that may conflict with opaque AI recommendations.

A single global deployment may need jurisdiction-specific modifications. The cost of compliance multiplies with each jurisdiction. The risk of non-compliance multiplies faster.

*The Machines That Cannot Be Replaced*

*"We've got insulin pumps from 2015 that can't be patched, running firmware that hasn't been updated in five years, now feeding data to an AI system that makes dosing recommendations. Every security person I know is terrified. But the pumps still work, replacing them costs millions, and the AI actually catches dosing errors. So we hold our breath and hope."*

— Health System Chief Information Security Officer (CISO)

The pump is still working. That's the problem. A device that fails gets replaced. A device that works persists: even when its operating system contains vulnerabilities published years ago, even when its protocols transmit data without encryption, even when every security assessment recommends decommissioning. The hospital has three thousand connected devices from dozens of manufacturers, spanning multiple generations of technology. The oldest devices predate the assumption that medical equipment would ever connect to networks.

The AI platform synthesizing data from these devices creates a single point of compromise for all of them. An attacker who penetrates your analytics layer gains access to every device feeding it data, and influence over clinical decisions affecting patients using those devices.

Electronic health record platforms dominate American healthcare. Epic, Oracle Health, and Meditech serve as the central nervous system for clinical operations. They are becoming what Habib described: an AI nervous system watching everything, understanding it in real time, coordinating the best next actions so the organization operates as one. But they were designed as comprehensive platforms for human users, not as AI integration substrates.

EHR APIs were designed for specific integration use cases: connecting laboratory systems, enabling patient portals, and transmitting prescriptions. They weren't designed for the broad data access that AI training and inference require. Health systems building AI capabilities find themselves working around API limitations, creating custom interfaces, negotiating with vendors for enhanced access that standard contracts don't provide. EHR implementations represent billions of dollars and years of customization. Switching vendors is difficult. This gives vendors leverage. If they don't want to enable AI capabilities that might compete with their own offerings, organizations have limited alternatives.

The AI that could transform healthcare operates at the mercy of platforms designed before AI was possible, controlled by vendors whose business interests may not align with the organizations deploying AI or the patients whose care depends on it.

FDA-regulated devices must maintain their approved configurations. Connecting a regulated device to an AI analytics platform raises questions about whether the integration affects the device's regulatory status. The manufacturer can't issue a security patch: every modification to a regulated device may require regulatory review. A vulnerability might persist for months or years while the manufacturer develops and validates a patch that doesn't affect clinical functionality.

The infusion pump adjusting medication delivery based on network commands. The cardiac monitor transmitting patient data wirelessly. The imaging equipment receiving configuration updates over the internet. Each device represents an attack surface that AI convergence is now connecting to central analytics platforms.

Data fragmentation compounds the infrastructure challenge. The same condition might be documented differently by different providers, coded differently in different systems, captured with different levels of detail in different contexts. The most clinically relevant information lives in unstructured data: clinical notes, radiology reports, and pathology findings, all free text that AI must interpret through natural language processing. When a patient moves between healthcare systems, their information transfers imperfectly.

Federal policy pushes toward greater interoperability: Fast Healthcare Interoperability Resources (FHIR) provides standardized APIs, health information exchanges aggregate data from multiple sources, information blocking rules prohibit organizations from unreasonably preventing sharing. The progress is uneven. FHIR adoption is incomplete. The infrastructure that could enable AI integration exists in partial, inconsistent form.

*The Hospital That Cannot Stop*

The ransomware deploys at 3:47 AM on a Saturday, the timing chosen because weekend staffing is thin and response will be slow.

By 4:15 AM, the electronic health record system is encrypted. The laboratory system is down. The pharmacy system won't dispense medications. The clinical decision to support AI that helps physicians catch dangerous drug interactions, identify deteriorating patients, and prioritize urgent cases has gone dark.

Your hospital cannot go offline while systems recover. Patients continue arriving. The emergency department sees 200 visits daily; they don't stop because the computers failed. The surgical schedule has procedures that can't be postponed: the cancer that needs removal, the cardiac bypass planned for weeks, the trauma patient who just came through the door. Manual procedures activate. Nurses write medication orders on paper. Physicians dictate notes for later transcription. The hospital that ran on integrated systems now runs on institutional memory, maintained by staff who remember how things used to work. Some of that staff retired years ago. The procedures exist in binders that haven't been opened since the last drill. The drill happened two years ago.

The ransomware operators offer the decryption key for $4.2 million in cryptocurrency. The FBI advises against paying. The hospital's cyber insurance has a $3 million cap and a deductible that wipes out the remaining coverage. The precedents are brutal. Universal Health Services absorbed an estimated $67 million impact from a 2020 attack. Scripps Health spent months recovering in 2021. CommonSpirit's 2022 breach spread across multiple states for weeks. Every case meant the same thing on the ground: delayed procedures, diverted ambulances, degraded care. Double extortion has evolved the threat: not just encrypting systems but stealing data and threatening release. The hospital faces two pressures at once. Restore operations or patient care degrades; prevent disclosure or patient privacy is violated on a massive scale.

AI convergence creates new ransomware targets. The platform integrating clinical decision support, documentation assistance, and operational analytics becomes a high-value target whose compromise affects multiple functions simultaneously. Unlike traditional data systems where encryption affects stored information, AI systems whose models are encrypted or corrupted may be irrecoverable. You can restore a database from backup. You can't restore an AI model that took months to train on proprietary clinical data. The data comes back. The learning doesn't. The model isn't data. It's learned patterns that exist only in mathematical weights. Encrypt those weights and the learning is lost.

The attack that may prove most dangerous doesn't look like an attack at all. A clinical decision support system at a regional medical center begins receiving training data updates through normal channels. The updates include subtle corruptions: medication interaction warnings that are slightly less sensitive than they should be, risk scores that underweight certain patient characteristics, diagnostic suggestions that drift toward less aggressive workups. Each individual change is small enough to escape notice. The aggregate effect, accumulated over months, is a system that misses drug interactions it should catch, underestimates risk in patients who should be flagged, recommends against imaging studies that would have found early cancers.

The adversary compromised the data pipeline feeding the AI, introducing poison that looked like normal training updates. The system continued functioning. Its performance metrics remained acceptable. The harm manifested in patients who received subtly wrong care, distributed across thousands of encounters, invisible to any monitoring not specifically designed to detect it. By the time the poisoning was discovered, the corrupted model had influenced eighteen months of clinical decisions. Calculating the harm required reviewing every case where the AI's recommendation might have been affected, an impossible task for a system that touches every patient encounter. The medical center's response involved decommissioning the AI, reverting to pre-AI clinical workflows while a replacement was developed. The efficiency gains of three years evaporated overnight. The harm from eighteen months of corrupted recommendations could never be fully assessed.

Healthcare data commands premium prices on criminal markets because it cannot be changed when compromised. A credit card number can be invalidated. A Social Security number can be monitored. A medical history endures. One comprehensive record fuels several fraud schemes at once: medical identity theft to obtain care under a false identity, insurance fraud using legitimate patient information, and identity theft leveraging the personally identifiable information health records contain. The value persists indefinitely. Attackers can hold stolen healthcare data for years, waiting for opportunities to monetize it. AI convergence multiplies this value. Systems that synthesize comprehensive patient information create consolidated targets. Rather than stealing records piecemeal, an attacker who compromises an AI platform accesses synthesized information about entire patient populations.

Nation-states target healthcare for intelligence purposes. Pharmaceutical research proved its value during COVID-19, with documented attempts by Chinese and Russian actors to steal research. Health data about specific high-value individuals supports espionage operations. Pandemic preparedness intelligence helps adversaries understand capabilities and vulnerabilities. AI systems that consolidate research data or analyze healthcare system capacity become attractive intelligence targets. The synthesis that enables clinical insight enables intelligence collection with equal efficiency.

The attack vectors keep expanding. Training data poisoning corrupts healthcare AI to cause systematic harm. Prompt injection manipulates clinical AI through crafted inputs. Patient-provided information flows directly into AI systems, and if patients can be recruited or coerced into providing malicious inputs, prompt injection becomes a clinical attack vector. Adversarial examples fool medical imaging AI: subtle modifications to images, invisible to human viewers, make the AI miss tumors, misidentify conditions, and generate incorrect measurements.

The compliance officer returns to the auditor two weeks later. Her research found no clear answer. HIPAA guidance doesn't address AI synthesis. Case law doesn't exist yet. Regulatory interpretation is evolving.

She presents the hospital's interpretation: synthesis for treatment purposes is authorized under the treatment authorization, provided patients are notified that AI analysis occurs. She documents the interpretation, the reasoning, the regulatory provisions it relies on. The documentation won't prevent enforcement action if regulators later disagree. It will demonstrate good faith. It will provide a basis for arguing that penalties should be limited. It will show the organization tried to comply with rules that don't clearly exist.

This is what compliance looks like in healthcare AI: documenting interpretations of ambiguous requirements, engaging with regulators to shape frameworks still being developed, building beyond minimum requirements in hopes that future rules will validate current practices, monitoring regulatory evolution because guidance can change with little notice. The maze has no map. The organizations inside it navigate by judgment, hoping their judgment aligns with interpretations that haven't been issued yet. The patient whose care depends on that AI system has no way to know whether the organization using it is compliant or not. The rules that would tell them don't exist in clear enough form to answer the question.

# Chapter 14: The Drill That Happened Two Years Ago

The challenges documented throughout this section might seem to argue against healthcare AI adoption altogether. The hallucination risks, consent paradoxes, time-pressure constraints, bias amplification, regulatory uncertainty, legacy complexity, diverse threats, professional culture disruption: each represents genuine danger.

But that option isn't available. AI convergence in healthcare is proceeding regardless. It will proceed thoughtfully or recklessly.

*Without Governance That Works*

Without cross-functional AI oversight, you're making decisions no single perspective can evaluate. IT understands the technology but not the clinical implications. Clinicians understand patient care but not the security risks. Legal understands liability but not the technical constraints. Each perspective sees part of the problem. No one sees all of it.

The AI that seems clinically valuable may violate regulations no one on the approval chain understood. The AI that seems technically sound may introduce clinical risks engineers never considered. Cross-functional committees don't slow down AI deployment because bureaucracy demands it. They slow it down because every deployment involves tradeoffs no single perspective can evaluate.

Without genuine authority, these committees become advisory bodies whose recommendations can be overruled by executives under competitive pressure. The governance that could have caught the problem becomes theater.

Without a clinical AI review processes, your organization treats AI differently than other clinical interventions. A new medication requires clinical trials, pharmacy committee review, formulary decision. AI that influences clinical decisions gets deployed because the vendor demonstrated capability and the competitor already bought it. The review that would have asked "for whom does this AI work, and for whom does it fail?" doesn't happen. The bias that harms specific patient populations goes undetected until patients are harmed.

If your organization does not monitor AI after deployment, you validate once and assume the validation persists. Model drift goes undetected. Performance degradation accumulates. Bias emerges as the patient population shifts. The AI that worked when deployed works differently now, and no one knows it.

*The Market That Sells Governance Back to You*

The governance vacuum does not go unnoticed by vendors. It goes unnoticed by patients.

Healthcare AI governance has become a lucrative product category. Clinical AI monitoring platforms promise to track model performance, detect drift, flag bias, and generate the documentation that regulators and accreditors will eventually demand. As a service, bias auditing firms now sell the disaggregated performance analysis that Chapter 11 identified as essential and that Chapter 14 acknowledged most organizations cannot perform internally. HIPAA-AI compliance consultants market readiness assessments for regulatory frameworks that do not yet exist in final form.

Some of these services address genuine needs. The disaggregated bias analysis that a community hospital cannot perform alone may be achievable through a specialized firm with the statistical expertise and benchmark data to do it properly. A clinical AI monitoring platform that tracks model performance across patient populations provides value no manual process can replicate at scale.

The problem is distinguishing genuine capability from repackaged familiarity. The HIPAA compliance firm that has conducted privacy risk assessments for fifteen years now offers "AI-ready HIPAA assessments." The assessment maps AI deployment onto existing HIPAA requirements and produces documentation, while leaving inference attacks, consent paradoxes, and the synthesis problems Chapter 10 documented unaddressed. The hospital passes the assessment. The patient whose psychiatric history is reconstructable from prescription timing patterns is no more protected than before.

EHR vendors occupy a particularly conflicted position. Epic, Oracle Health, and Meditech control the platforms through which most clinical AI reaches physicians. They are simultaneously the infrastructure providers, the AI capability developers, and increasingly the governance solution sellers. The vendor that activates AI features by default, the dynamic identified earlier in this chapter, now offers governance tools to manage the features it activated without asking. The organization that should be governing its AI vendor is purchasing governance from that same vendor. The conflict is structural, not malicious. It is also unresolved.

The test for healthcare is clinical, not administrative. Does the monitoring platform detect the kind of hallucination described in Chapter 10, the 94% confidence score for a cancer that does not exist? Does the bias audit reveal the patterns Chapter 11 documented: the algorithm that systematically underserves populations whose historical care was already inadequate? Does the compliance assessment address what happens when AI inference reconstructs information patients deliberately withheld, or does it simply confirm that the existing consent forms contain the word "artificial intelligence"?

The organization that can answer these questions is governing its AI. The organization that purchased a platform to answer them for it is governing its vendor relationship. These are not the same activity. The patients cannot tell the difference until the harm has already occurred.

*Without Integration That Protects*

Leadership that doesn't clearly identify AI recommendations as such leaves clinicians unable to evaluate what they're seeing. The recommendation appears to come from the system, indistinguishable from other information. The clinician who would have questioned an AI-generated suggestion accepts it because it looks like established clinical guidance. Transparency isn't a bureaucratic requirement. It's the foundation for appropriate skepticism.

A hospital that doesn't require friction for high-stakes decisions enables reflexive acceptance. The cancer diagnosis, the surgical recommendation, the end-of-life care decision. All of them flow through workflows designed for efficiency rather than deliberation. The eleven minutes don't include time to independently evaluate the AI's reasoning. A checkbox that says "I reviewed this recommendation" provides legal cover without ensuring review actually occurred. Friction that requires genuine attestation creates the pause that enables judgment.

If you make overriding AI difficult, you create clinicians who accept recommendations they doubt. If disagreeing with the AI requires extensive documentation, multiple approvals, or explanations to supervisors tracking override rates, clinicians follow the algorithm to avoid the burden. The path to independent judgment must be at least as smooth as the path to acceptance. Otherwise, human oversight becomes human rubber-stamping. And the younger clinicians? They'll figure out the shortcuts before anyone else.

*Without Preparation for Failure*

You don't realize how much AI failure planning matters until you're in the middle of an incident and discover you never made one. The ransomware encrypts the clinical decision support system at 3:47 AM on a Saturday. The manual procedures exist in binders that haven't been opened since the last drill. The drill happened two years ago. The staff who remembered how to practice without AI support have retired.

Graceful degradation planning isn't pessimism. It's recognition that every system fails eventually.

Hospitals that don't maintain staff skills for AI-less practice finds those skills have atrophied when they're needed. The nurses have been following AI alerts for five years. The physicians have been accepting AI diagnostic suggestions for a decade. The manual capabilities that would enable continued operations during AI failure exist only in professionals who learned medicine before AI was possible.

Training on manual procedures, drills without AI support, and operational practices that maintain human situational awareness are not inefficiencies to be eliminated. They're the preservation of capability that will be needed when the AI fails on the worst possible day.

Knowledge transfer matters just as much. Institutional memory must be captured before it walks out the door: the reasons clinical protocols exist, the history behind treatment exceptions, the judgment that never made it into documentation.

The nurse who knows that a specific combination of vital sign changes precedes sepsis thirty minutes before the textbook says so. The pharmacist who remembers why a particular drug interaction warning was added after a near-miss five years ago. The radiologist who knows that the scanner in Suite 3 produces slightly different contrast profiles than the one in Suite 5. This knowledge lives in human minds. Lose it, and you're operating blind when AI fails.

*When You're Not the Academic Medical Center*

The scenarios in this part describe academic medical centers, regional health systems, hospitals with Chief Medical Information Officers and AI governance committees. The diagnostic AI that hallucinated pancreatic cancer was caught at a major teaching hospital where a pathologist thought to question the system. Mrs. Chen's eleven-minute appointment happened in a practice with access to specialists who could have provided a second opinion.

Most healthcare operates differently.

The critical access hospital with twenty-five beds serves a rural county where the nearest specialist is ninety minutes away. The independent primary care practice runs on an EHR platform whose AI features were activated by default in the last update. The community health center treats patients in twelve languages with a technology budget that covers the EHR license and not much else. The skilled nursing facility's AI exposure arrives entirely through the medication management system its pharmacy benefit manager selected.

These facilities face the same convergence dynamics as the academic medical center: the same hallucination risks, the same bias patterns, the same erosion of clinical autonomy. Here they arrive amplified by constraints it does not share.

Dr. Okonkwo's eleven minutes become seven in a federally qualified health center where panel sizes are larger and reimbursement rates are lower. The automation bias that makes a teaching hospital physician defer to a 94% confidence score is stronger when the physician has no colleague down the hall to consult, no tumor board meeting next Tuesday, no institutional culture of questioning algorithmic outputs. The rural physician who doubts the AI's recommendation may have no practical way to obtain an independent evaluation. The AI becomes not an advisor but the only advisor.

The bias documented in Chapter 11 hits harder here. The Optum algorithm that systematically underselected Black patients for care management operated across the healthcare system, but its effects concentrated where resources were already scarce. Community health centers serving predominantly minority populations had the least capacity to detect algorithmic bias, the least leverage to demand vendor transparency, and the least ability to perform the disaggregated performance analysis that would reveal the problem. The patients the algorithm didn't see were disproportionately patients the system was already failing.

The consent paradoxes deepen. An academic medical center might employ a privacy officer who understands that AI inference can reconstruct information patients chose not to share. A twenty-five-bed hospital relies on a compliance consultant who visits quarterly. The inference attacks described in Chapter 10 are technically identical in both settings: psychiatric diagnoses reconstructed from prescription patterns, HIV status inferred from appointment scheduling. The ability to detect, prevent, or even recognize them is not.

Resource-constrained healthcare organizations share the strategic options outlined in the prior book: concentrate vendor relationships, choose vendors serving larger systems whose enterprise customers negotiate security standards, document AI-influenced decisions rigorously. For healthcare, three additional principles matter.

First, treat clinical override documentation as both a safety mechanism and a legal defense. Every time a clinician departs from an AI recommendation, the reason should be recorded. This creates a feedback loop that reveals where the AI performs poorly for the patient population actually being served, which may differ from the population the model was trained on. It also creates a record that demonstrates clinical judgment was exercised, not abdicated. Maria's override in room 412 should have been recorded as clinical excellence, not protocol deviation. Until hospitals build systems that recognize the difference, the documentation itself becomes the defense.

Second, demand transparency from EHR vendors about which features incorporate AI and what data those features access. Many clinicians in small practices do not know which of their workflow tools are AI-driven. They cannot exercise oversight over systems they do not know exist. The EHR vendor that activates AI features by default without clear disclosure has made a choice about clinical autonomy that belongs to the clinician, not the vendor.

Third, use existing peer networks for what mutual aid provides in critical infrastructure. State medical associations, specialty societies, and health information exchanges, which are the structures through which small practices can share incident experiences, identify AI performance problems across similar patient populations, and collectively pressure vendors in ways individual practices cannot. The rural physician who discovers the AI consistently misreads imaging from her facility's older equipment needs a channel to share that finding. Without it, the same failure repeats in every similar facility, invisible to each.

The gap between what AI convergence demands of healthcare and what resource-constrained providers can deliver is not a technology problem. It is a structural one. The community hospital adopting AI through its EHR vendor inherits the same risks as the academic medical center with none of the institutional infrastructure to manage them. Acknowledging this gap is the precondition both for addressing it and for ensuring that the patients who depend on these organizations do not bear the cost of risks no one told them existed.

*What This Reveals*

This is what the operational detail of the preceding chapters reveals: healthcare AI failures are not incidents to be aggregated and analyzed. They are injuries to individuals who came seeking help and received harm instead. The eleven minutes are not an abstraction about workflow efficiency. They are the interval in which a physician must decide whether to trust a blue box or trust themselves, knowing that the system measuring their performance rewards one choice and punishes the other. The buffer being thinned is not a process metric. It is the space in which human judgment could catch what the algorithm missed, closing visit by visit, innovation by innovation, until what remains cannot hold. And when it fails to hold, the person who pays is not the vendor, not the health system, not the physician whose time was too constrained to pause. It is the patient who trusted all of them.

Medicine has always learned from failure: through errors that revealed what wasn't known, through harms that motivated safer practice. AI convergence may not permit that model. The harms propagate through systems that touch every patient, amplified by the same efficiency that makes AI valuable. The organization that builds resilience before failure captures AI's benefits while managing its risks. The organization that waits to learn from failure may find that some lessons cannot be survived.

"The algorithm doesn't feel the weight of telling a patient they have cancer. The physician does, even when the algorithm made the call."

The algorithm will never feel it. The organizations that deploy it must.

Healthcare's lessons do not stay within healthcare. The same AI that hallucinates a diagnosis can hallucinate a credit risk assessment. The same bias that makes patients invisible can make borrowers invisible. The same time-pressure collapse that turns recommendations into decisions operates wherever AI meets high-stakes human judgment under operational constraint. What healthcare reveals in examination rooms and hospital beds, financial services will reveal on trading floors and lending offices, at speeds that make eleven minutes feel generous.

# Part IV : Financial Services

## Chapter 15: The Signature That Means Nothing

On May 6, 2010, the Dow Jones Industrial Average plunged nearly 1,000 points in minutes, then recovered almost as quickly. The "Flash Crash" erased and restored approximately $1 trillion in market value within an afternoon. Algorithmic trading systems interacting in ways no one had anticipated, feedback loops amplifying a relatively modest initial sell order into cascading collapse.

That happened with relatively simple algorithms operating at early-2010s speeds. Today's AI systems are more sophisticated, faster, more deeply integrated into financial operations. The potential for AI-related market disruption exceeds what 2010 demonstrated.

The recovery may not be as quick.

Critical infrastructure operates in seconds. Healthcare operates in minutes to hours. Financial services operates in milliseconds. This is not a matter of degree. It is a difference in kind.

A trading algorithm executes thousands of transactions before you recognize something is wrong. By the time your judgment engages, consequences have already cascaded through interconnected markets. At its core, financial services is information processing at industrial scale: databases with humans attached. Healthcare involves human bodies that require human touch. Critical infrastructure involves physical systems on physical timescales. Financial services is pure information, and its transformation by AI convergence is correspondingly total.

High-frequency trading systems execute decisions in microseconds: millionths of a second. The latency between market signal and trading response is measured in the time it takes light to travel a few dozen meters. Firms spend hundreds of millions of dollars to shave microseconds from response times: co-located servers positioned physically closer to exchange matching engines, custom network hardware bypassing standard protocols, fiber optic routes approximating geodesics between financial centers.

At these speeds, you cannot review individual decisions. You cannot examine each order before submission; by the time neural signals travel from eyes to brain to hands, thousands of opportunities have passed. The algorithms operate autonomously not by choice but by necessity.

*"I sign off on strategies I cannot fully understand, deployed at speeds I cannot perceive, making decisions I cannot review. My signature on the approval document is a legal fiction that everyone, the regulators, the board, me, pretends is meaningful oversight. We all know better. We do it anyway because the alternative is admitting that no one is actually in control."*

— Head of Algorithmic Trading, Tier 1 Investment Bank

Traditional algorithmic trading executes predefined strategies: if price crosses threshold X, buy quantity Y. Sophisticated, but rule-based. AI trading systems learn strategies from data, identifying patterns human designers might never specify. They adapt to changing market conditions in ways deterministic algorithms cannot. This adaptability is precisely what makes them valuable. And precisely what makes them dangerous.

A rule-based algorithm behaves predictably; its failure modes, while severe, are at least comprehensible. An AI system that learned its strategy from data may behave in ways no one, including its creators, fully understands. When that behavior goes wrong at microsecond speeds, consequences propagate throughout the financial system before anyone recognizes a problem exists.

Consider the timeline:

09:31:04.003 EST — Asian markets close with unexpected volatility in semiconductor futures. A model at a Chicago-based quantitative fund flags a correlation anomaly.

09:31:04.007 EST — Same model initiates protective hedge across 847 related instruments. Total elapsed time: 4 milliseconds.

09:31:04.012 EST — Hedge activity triggers pattern recognition at three competing funds running similar architectures trained on overlapping datasets. Each initiates its own protective response.

09:31:04.019 EST — Liquidity in affected instruments drops 34% as market makers' AI systems detect abnormal flow and widen spreads.

09:31:04.031 EST — First human operator sees alert on screen. By this point, 2,847 trades have executed across 12 exchanges. The cascade is 28 milliseconds old.

09:31:04.089 EST — Human operator reaches for phone to call risk desk. Total market value shifted: $2.3 billion. Circuit breakers have not engaged because no single instrument has moved enough to trigger them.

09:31:07.000 EST — Risk desk phone rings. The operator who answers is looking at data that is now three seconds stale: an eternity in which another 11,000 trades have executed.

The specific numbers are illustrative, but the dynamic plays out in some form every trading day. Such cascades are not in doubt; whether they remain contained is.

Every governance framework, every regulatory requirement, every risk management best practice assumes humans can intervene in consequential decisions. At microsecond timescales, this assumption is physically false. Yet regulatory frameworks still require human accountability. When an AI trading system causes losses, regulators expect to identify responsible humans. Who authorized the strategy? Who monitored its execution? Who failed to prevent the harm? These questions assume a model of decision-making that no longer applies. The strategy emerged from machine learning processes no individual fully specified. Monitoring was impossible at the speeds involved. Prevention would have required intervention in timeframes shorter than human reaction times.

The responses you have developed are none of them satisfactory. Pre-trade controls establish boundaries AI systems cannot exceed: position limits, loss thresholds, volatility triggers. Human oversight occurs in setting the boundaries, not reviewing decisions. But boundaries calibrated for normal conditions prove inadequate for the unusual conditions where human judgment matters most.

Kill switches provide emergency shutdown when AI behavior becomes clearly problematic. But by the time unusual activity becomes observable to humans, assessed as problematic, escalated to someone with authority, and acted upon, substantial damage has occurred.

Real-time monitoring sets AI to watch AI, using pattern recognition to detect anomalies and alert human operators. But monitoring AI can fail the same ways trading AI fails. If both learned from similar data, they share blind spots.

The velocity that defines financial services creates security vulnerabilities other sectors do not face at comparable intensity. In markets where microseconds matter, an attacker who can delay a competitor's market data, even slightly, can trade on information the competitor has not yet received. Latency arbitrage is a documented strategy. The line between aggressive trading and market manipulation depends on intent that proves difficult to establish. AI systems learning optimal timing strategies may inadvertently learn latency exploitation techniques. The AI does not know it is doing something problematic; it knows certain timing patterns correlate with better outcomes.

Markets operate globally around the clock. Human attention does not. An adversary can time attacks to maximize the window before human response, striking when monitoring is thinnest: overnight hours in a firm's home time zone, weekend periods, holiday coverage.

Your AI does not sleep. Neither does the adversary's.

*The War That Operates at the Same Speed*

Speed does not merely create vulnerability in legitimate operations. It arms the adversaries exploiting them.

Consider what happened at 14:23:17 GMT. A CFO at a mid-sized manufacturing company received a video call from what appeared to be the company's CEO, currently traveling in Singapore. The CEO's face, voice, and mannerisms were indistinguishable from reality. The "CEO" explained an urgent acquisition opportunity requiring immediate wire transfer. The conversation included inside references to last week's board meeting, information scraped from an executive's compromised email. By 14:27:44, the CFO had initiated a $4.7 million transfer, following what appeared to be proper authorization protocol. The deepfake AI had successfully mimicked not just appearance but decision-making style, addressing the CFO's procedural objections before she raised them. The transfer cleared initial fraud screening. The amount was unusual but within authorization limits, and the behavioral biometrics on the CFO's workstation showed normal patterns because she was behaving normally, believing she was following legitimate instructions. By 14:47:33, funds had moved through three intermediate accounts and converted to cryptocurrency. The real CEO was unreachable, his phone spoofed to show him calling from Singapore.

Recovery was already impossible.

This is not hypothetical. A Hong Kong finance worker transferred $25 million after participating in a video call with what appeared to be multiple company executives, all AI-generated deepfakes. The attack succeeded because it combined multiple seemingly independent verifications: the request came from known contacts, in a familiar meeting format, with multiple apparent participants. Each element reinforced the others' apparent legitimacy.

Financial fraud has always evolved, but AI-native fraud represents something categorically different. Manual fraud was labor-intensive and could not scale: forged signatures, altered checks, impersonation. Automated fraud let attacks target thousands with minimal marginal effort: card skimming, phishing campaigns, credential stuffing. Adaptive fraud used machine learning to optimize attacks, learning which targets were vulnerable and how to evade specific detection. AI-native fraud goes further: attacks designed and executed by AI systems with minimal human involvement. The AI generates convincing content, identifies optimal targets, times attacks for maximum effectiveness, adapts in real time to defensive responses. Human fraudsters specify objectives and parameters. The attack itself is increasingly autonomous.

Deepfake impersonation extends beyond the video calls that made headlines. Financial services now faces voice deepfakes in which relationship managers seem to call clients, and synthetic identities combining real and fabricated information to create personas that pass verification. Synthetic identity fraud is particularly challenging because there is no victim to report it. Real people whose identities are stolen notice and complain. Synthetic identities exist only for fraudulent purposes: credit-building patiently over months, then executing fraud and vanishing. Detection must identify them proactively, without the trigger of victim complaints.

Personalized social engineering uses AI to craft attacks tailored to individual targets: not generic phishing emails, but communications referencing the target's actual projects, using language patterns matching legitimate correspondents, arriving at psychologically optimal times. Meanwhile, adversarial machine learning attacks target the AI systems institutions deploy for defense. If a bank uses machine learning to detect fraud, adversaries develop inputs specifically crafted to make fraudulent transactions appear legitimate to automated detection while remaining recognizably fraudulent to humans who never see them.

The contest between AI-powered fraud and AI-powered detection has no stable equilibrium. You must defend against all attack vectors. Attackers need only find one that works. The cost asymmetry is structural. Capability democratization puts sophisticated attack tools within reach of unsophisticated actors. Capabilities that once required nation-state resources now download from dark web marketplaces. Information asymmetry favors offense: fraudsters study publicly documented defenses, regulatory filings, academic papers. They probe systems systematically, learning defensive patterns without defenders knowing they are being mapped. Time pressure completes the disadvantage. Attackers choose when to strike, timing operations for low-coverage hours and high-volume periods when anomalies hide in noise.

Every defensive advance, from behavioral biometrics to network analysis to cross-channel detection, creates a new target for offensive innovation. Every offensive innovation demands a defensive response. The cycle has no endpoint.

You cannot win this war permanently. The realistic objective is making fraud expensive enough to deter many attackers and contain losses from those who persist. But "enough" is a moving target. What deters today's attackers may not deter tomorrow's.

The war cannot be won. It can only be fought, and surviving is itself a worthy struggle.

# Chapter 16: Dominoes at the Speed of Light

A sufficiently severe AI failure at your institution does not just damage your institution. It triggers cascading effects that threaten the broader financial system.

Modern financial services operates through dense networks of interconnection that enable efficiency while creating pathways for contagion. Counterparty relationships connect institutions through contractual obligations. A bank that fails to meet its obligations creates problems for counterparties, potentially affecting their ability to meet obligations to others. The 2008 financial crisis demonstrated how counterparty failures cascade: Lehman Brothers' bankruptcy created uncertainty about which institutions held exposure, freezing credit markets as firms refused to lend to counterparties whose health they could not assess.

AI convergence creates new counterparty dimensions. If multiple institutions depend on the same AI vendor, the vendor's failure affects all of them simultaneously. If institutions' AI systems learned from similar data, they make similar errors at the same time. The correlation in AI behavior creates correlation in institutional outcomes: exactly the systemic risk diversification is supposed to prevent.

*"The regulators ask us about our models. They never ask whether our models look like everyone else's models. That's the question that keeps me up at night. We've all been training on the same twenty years of market data. We've all been hiring from the same programs, using the same architectures,*

*validating against the same benchmarks. If we're wrong, we're all wrong together, and that's not a scenario anyone's stress-tested."*

— Chief Risk Officer, Global Asset Manager

If every major bank's credit risk AI was trained on data from the same benign economic period, they may all underestimate risk from conditions outside that period, and all at once. This correlation problem is invisible until it manifests. Each institution evaluates its own AI performance without visibility into competitors' AI. Each institution's AI may pass validation tests that assume independent errors. The systemic vulnerability becomes apparent only when stress conditions trigger correlated failures across institutions that all believed their AI was performing adequately.

Market interconnections link prices and behaviors across instruments, exchanges, and geographies. A disruption in one market affects related markets through arbitrage relationships, hedging activities, portfolio rebalancing. The Flash Crash began in equity index futures, spread to individual equities, affected exchange-traded funds, influenced options markets tied to all of the above. AI systems trading across markets learn these interconnection patterns. And they may amplify them. An AI that recognizes correlation between instruments trades both when signals suggest opportunity. If many AI systems learn similar cross-market patterns, their collective trading amplifies the very correlations they learned, creating feedback loops that did not exist before AI imposed them.

Algorithmic herding emerges when AI systems' learned strategies converge on similar behaviors. If many AI systems learn that certain market conditions warrant aggressive selling, they all sell aggressively when those conditions appear. That selling creates the price movement they anticipated and triggers further selling from systems with similar learned patterns. Human herding develops over hours or days. AI herding develops in milliseconds. By the time you see the stampede, it's already over. The compressed timeline means herding progresses from incipient to catastrophic before traditional circuit breakers engage. A traditional market maker might widen spreads during volatility, providing liquidity at a price compensating for uncertainty. An AI system that learned primarily from calm conditions might instead withdraw liquidity entirely: rational for the individual firm, catastrophic collectively.

Infrastructure dependencies compound the exposure. Financial services relies on shared systems: payment networks, clearinghouses, data providers, cloud platforms. AI convergence concentrates this dependency further. The cloud platforms hosting AI workloads serve multiple institutions. The specialized hardware running AI inference comes from limited suppliers. The data feeds training AI systems flow through chokepoints. An adversary targeting AI infrastructure can affect numerous institutions simultaneously.

The systemic risks do not respect national boundaries, yet regulatory frameworks remain jurisdictional. A cascade beginning in Asian markets during New York's overnight hours propagates through European markets before American regulators have finished their morning coffee. Coordination mechanisms exist in theory: the Financial Stability Board, bilateral regulatory agreements, information-sharing protocols. They operate at human speeds in a system moving at machine speeds. Stress testing requirements mandate institutions evaluate AI performance under adverse conditions, but defining stress scenarios for risks that have not yet materialized at scale requires imagining scenarios with no historical precedent. Getting the scenarios wrong produces false assurance rather than genuine insight.

Circuit breakers designed for human-speed trading may need to engage faster and more granularly, halting specific instruments or strategies before disruptions spread. But calibration is treacherous. Triggers set too easily create frequent disruptions reducing market efficiency. Triggers set too slowly fail to prevent cascades they were designed to stop. The optimal calibration depends on AI capabilities that continue evolving. What works today may be inadequate tomorrow.

Systemic risk creates a collective action problem with no clean solution. Your AI deployment decisions affect not just your institution but the broader system. Yet you have limited incentive to account for systemic effects that fall primarily on others. A firm deploying AI for trading captures the profits from successful strategies while externalizing systemic risks to the broader market. If everyone deploys similar AI and those systems collectively create fragility, the costs fall on all market participants, including those who did not deploy AI at all. Responsible institutions must develop internal frameworks for assessing systemic risk contributions even absent regulatory requirements. They should act not because regulators demand it but because systemic failures harm everyone. Including the institutions that triggered them.

*The Ancient Code Beneath the Tower*

The cascades described above do not propagate through modern, well-mapped infrastructure. They propagate through systems whose foundations no one fully understands.

*"I've been here twenty-three years, and I'm one of maybe four people who understand how the overnight batch reconciliation actually works. The documentation says one thing; the system does something different that someone changed in 1997 to fix an issue we no longer remember. When I retire next year, that knowledge leaves with me. The AI team wants to 'modernize' this process. They have no idea what they're touching."*

— Senior Systems Analyst, Major U.S. Bank

Major financial institutions run core systems originally built in the Common Business-Oriented Language (COBOL) during the 1960s and 1970s. These systems process trillions of dollars in transactions daily with reliability rates modern systems struggle to match. They represent decades of accumulated business logic, edge case handling, and institutional knowledge encoded in millions of lines of code. They persist not because institutions are ignorant of modern technology, but because replacing them carries enormous risk.

Core banking systems are integrated with everything else the bank does. They embed business rules that escape complete documentation. They handle edge cases discovered over decades of operation. Replacing them means replacing institutional memory. Much of that memory has become inaccessible.

The challenge is not that these systems are bad. They are remarkably robust. The challenge is that they were designed for a world of discrete transactions, clear audit trails, and human-speed processing. AI convergence demands synthesis across these systems in ways their designers never contemplated.

COBOL systems typically lack the APIs that modern integration assumes. Extracting data for AI training may require batch processes that introduce latency. Real-time AI inference may need to wait for batch windows rather than operating continuously. The temporal patterns of legacy systems constrain the real-time ambitions of AI convergence.

More dangerously, AI learns from the data it receives. When that data flows through legacy systems, AI learns patterns that exist for reasons no one remembers. The batch timing that exists because of a near-miss incident in 1983. The sequence prohibition that exists because of a fraud case in 1991. The workaround that exists because a vendor went bankrupt in 2002. The AI does not know these reasons. It learns the patterns as given, then optimizes in ways that can reverse protections no one remembers creating.

Decades of technology evolution have created integration architectures of extraordinary complexity. Each new system added over the years required connections to existing systems. Each merger or acquisition brought additional systems that had to be integrated. Each regulatory requirement created new data flows. The result, at many institutions, is a tangle of point-to-point integrations, message queues, file transfers, and API calls beyond any one person's grasp.

Data flows through these connections in patterns that have evolved organically rather than through intentional design. Data lineage, which tracks where data came from and how it was transformed, may be impossible to reconstruct for information that has flowed through multiple legacy integration paths.

Each integration point is a potential vulnerability. Legacy integrations may use protocols without modern security features. The complexity makes comprehensive security assessment nearly impossible. There are too many connections to verify.

Today's most common approach to this integration challenge is Retrieval-Augmented Generation (RAG), and it epitomizes the problem. RAG allows an AI to fetch documents from these legacy stores and synthesize answers from them, but the retrieval still assumes information lives in discrete locations with discrete permissions. It is a bolt-on bridge between the database era and the convergence era, and like every bolt-on described in this book, it inherits the security assumptions of the old architecture while enabling the synthesis capabilities of the new one, governing neither.

And the humans who understand these systems are aging out of the workforce. COBOL programmers who built them in the 1970s have retired or will soon. The institutional knowledge about why systems work the way they do leaves with them. Much was never written down. Some was written down and lost. Some exists in documentation that no longer matches reality.

Meanwhile, AI convergence requires machine learning engineering, data science, and AI security. Those skills exist in a talent market that financial services competes for with technology companies offering different cultures, compensation structures, and work environments. You need both: people who understand why the legacy systems work the way they do, and people who can build AI systems that integrate with them safely. The first group is disappearing. The second group has options.

The tower stands on ancient code. The people who understand that code are leaving. And nobody thought to ask them where the load-bearing walls are. The people building the new floors have never seen the foundation. And the dominoes, when they fall, will fall through every floor at once.

# Chapter 17: The Fictions We Tell Regulators

Financial regulation assumes transactions and decisions can be traced to responsible parties. This assumption developed when humans made decisions and could explain their reasoning.

AI makes this assumption false.

> *"The regulators want us to explain why the model denied a loan. The honest answer is 'because of a complex interaction of 847 features weighted through 12 hidden layers that we cannot decompose into human-interpretable factors.' That's not an answer they can accept. So we generate a post-hoc explanation that sounds reasonable, top factors contributing to the decision, knowing full well it's an approximation at best. At worst it's a fiction we tell to satisfy a regulatory requirement that assumes decisions still work the way they used to."*

— Chief Compliance Officer, Regional Bank

Fair lending laws require explainable credit decisions. "The AI determined you were too risky" is not compliant. A neural network approving or denying credit based on billions of parameters cannot explain why in terms satisfying regulatory expectations. This is the audit trail paradox: traditional compliance assumes decisions can be traced backward to specific inputs, specific rules, specific responsible parties. AI decisions emerge from billions of parameters interacting in ways no decomposition can faithfully represent. The audit trail that regulators require and that organizations document may bear little relationship to what the AI actually did. The explanations you provide are not windows into AI reasoning. They are reconstructions: plausible stories generated after the fact to satisfy requirements designed for a different kind of decision-making.

The model did not consider "top factors." It considered all factors simultaneously, weighted through mathematical operations no human designed or can fully interpret.

Everyone involved knows it might be AI magic: the compliance officers drafting the explanations, the regulators reviewing them, the auditors signing off. Why would anyone say it out loud? The fiction is load-bearing.

Continuous learning makes this worse. The model that made a decision six months ago may no longer exist in the form that made that decision. If regulators investigate, what should they examine? The current model? A historical version? The decision process as it existed at the time?

Model versioning requirements, which maintain historical states for potential examination, add substantial operational complexity. But storing model weights is not enough. Reconstructing the inference environment requires the data preprocessing, feature engineering, and operational context that produced the decision. Most institutions cannot do this reliably. But the appearance of audit capability? That they can maintain. Why would substance matter when no one's looking that closely?

When AI synthesizes information across multiple sources to reach conclusions, attributing outcomes to specific inputs becomes impossible. If an AI trading system lost money, was the loss due to market data, model architecture, training data, or real-time inputs? The synthesis process combines all of these. Isolating the responsible element may not be achievable even in principle. Accountability requires traceability. AI architecturally defeats traceability. The governance problem is not that institutions are hiding something. It is that there may be nothing coherent to find.

Financial services operates under regulatory frameworks spanning jurisdictions with incompatible requirements. The EU's AI Act classifies financial services AI as "high-risk," requiring conformity assessments, human oversight, and documentation exceeding U.S. requirements. GDPR grants explanation rights. U.S. fair lending laws require adverse action explanations. Asian frameworks have their own expectations.

An AI system must provide different explanation types for different jurisdictions, each already a fiction in its home regulatory context and now multiplied across incompatible frameworks.

Data localization requirements restrict where data can be processed, potentially preventing the cross-border synthesis that creates AI convergence's efficiency benefits. An AI system trained on data from Europe, refined in Asia, hosted in North America, and queried globally may be compliant nowhere and exposed everywhere.

Comprehensive logging must capture inputs, outputs, model versions, and decision context: a significant engineering undertaking for systems where every millisecond matters. Retention requirements vary; some jurisdictions mandate multi-year storage of decision records that institutions cannot meaningfully reconstruct.

The gap between what AI does and what explanations capture remains unresolved. Institutions navigate this gap through careful documentation, probabilistic compliance, and the collective understanding that everyone is pretending. The pretense holds until it does not.

*The Governors of the Invisible*

The fiction extends beyond what institutions tell regulators. It extends to what institutions tell themselves about who is governing these systems.

*"Five years ago, I managed a team of forty analysts doing transaction monitoring. Today I manage eight, plus three AI systems. The work is better, we catch more, with fewer false positives. But those thirty-two people? They knew things. They had judgment. They remembered patterns from cases years ago. The AI doesn't remember. It doesn't have judgment. It has parameters. And when something new happens, something the training data never saw, I have eight people trying to do what forty used to do, and an AI that's confidently wrong."*

— Senior Compliance Officer, Global Bank

Of the three sectors examined in this book, financial services experiences the fastest and most extensive workforce displacement. The sector is information processing at industrial scale. AI performs core functions that employ millions: processing transactions, assessing risk, detecting fraud, interacting with customers. Trading floors that once employed thousands now operate with dozens overseeing automated systems. Back-office operations run with minimal human intervention. The pace accelerates. Loan underwriting. Compliance review. Advisory services. Each falls within AI capabilities. Each reduction in headcount represents jobs eliminated, and judgment lost.

You become a governor of systems you cannot perceive. You set parameters for AI that operates at speeds beyond human comprehension. You review outcomes you cannot have influenced in real time. You sign approvals for strategies you cannot fully understand, deployed at velocities you cannot observe, making decisions you cannot review. Your signature says you're accountable. Your calendar says you had eleven minutes.

The Chicago trader described in Part IV, staring at an anomaly flag she has never overridden, calling a supervisor who has never overridden it either, escalating until the window closes, embodies the paradox every sector faces.

The skill atrophy is dangerous because AI failures often correlate with crisis conditions: exactly when human skills matter most. The AI trained on normal market conditions fails during stress events.

Financial employees have direct access to value. A disgruntled employee who knows they are being replaced, understands exactly how money moves, and has credentials providing access creates risk that standard controls may not address. The insider threat intensifies because displacement is happening at scale, affecting workers who understand systems intimately and can see their own obsolescence approaching. Enhanced monitoring during workforce transitions must balance security against privacy rights, and against the risk that aggressive monitoring creates the resentment it tries to detect. The surveillance intended to catch the disgruntled insider may create them.

Institutional knowledge accumulated over decades resides in human minds. Why systems work as they do. Incidents that shaped practices. Regulatory relationships. Much is tacit rather than explicit: intuitions about risk, pattern recognition from experience, understanding of how the institution actually operates versus organizational charts. Institutions pursuing aggressive displacement may discover they have lost knowledge essential for situations AI was not trained to handle. The knowledge gap reveals itself only when the crisis arrives. By then the people who would have recognized the pattern are gone.

Financial services culture emphasizes performance metrics and competitive pressure. This drives rapid AI adoption, since anything that improves returns or reduces costs faces minimal resistance. But it also drives security shortcuts when controls are perceived as friction that reduces performance. Making security part of the performance equation, ensuring risk-adjusted returns account for AI security risks, requires culture change beyond compliance checkboxes. The institutions building this culture are positioned for sustainable AI adoption.

The others are positioned for the next regulatory response to the next crisis.

When the pretense finally collapses, when a decision causes harm significant enough to warrant genuine investigation, the audit trail leads to weights and gradients. The accountability framework points to mathematics. The responsible human is whoever signed the approval document for a system they could not audit, built by vendors who would not explain it.

Their signature meant nothing. Everyone knew. They signed anyway.

*The Industry Built on the Fiction*

The signature means nothing. But it generates enormous revenue for the ecosystem that makes it possible to sign.

The AI Security-Commercial Complex that *The AI Convergence Trap* identified in general terms manifests in financial services with particular force. The sector has the deepest compliance culture, the largest governance budgets, and the longest history of purchasing assurance from third parties. The infrastructure for buying confidence already exists. AI convergence gives it new products to sell.

Model risk management platforms promise SR 11-7 compliance for AI systems. They offer model inventories, validation workflows, documentation generation, and audit trail management. The capabilities are real, and they address the administrative dimension of model governance. What they do not address is whether the models being governed actually behave as documented. The inventory records the model. The validation workflow processes the paperwork. The audit trail logs the approvals. The model itself may have drifted since validation, may perform differently for demographics the validation dataset underrepresented, may interact with other models in ways no individual validation captured. The governance platform governs the documentation. The model governs the decisions. These are parallel activities that the platform's dashboard presents as one.

RegTech vendors sell automated compliance for AI-driven lending, trading, and fraud detection. The automation generates the adverse action notices fair lending requires, the transaction monitoring reports BSA/AML demands, the model performance documentation examiners expect. The generation is efficient. The notices are the post-hoc explanations the chief compliance officer described as fictions. Whether they accurately reflect what the AI actually did is a question the automation does not ask, and has no reason to. The fiction is the product.

The Big Four and major consulting firms have rebranded Governance, Risk, and Compliance (GRC) practices as "AI governance advisory." The partners leading these engagements understand regulatory expectations. They built their careers navigating Sarbanes-Oxley, Basel III, Dodd-Frank. They know what examiners want to see. Whether they understand what the AI systems they are governing actually do is a different question: how gradient descent produces decisions, how embedding spaces create inference risks, how adversarial inputs exploit model architectures. The deliverable is a framework. The framework maps AI operations to regulatory expectations. The mapping satisfies examiners. The AI-specific risks that exist outside those expectations, which no regulation has yet named, remain unaddressed and undocumented.

The financial services institution now faces a layered commercial dependency: the AI vendor that built the model, the model risk management platform that documents it, the RegTech vendor that automates its compliance reporting, and the consulting firm that designed the governance framework. Each layer adds cost. Each layer adds the appearance of control. The failure modes documented in Chapters 15 through 17 are the Flash Crash dynamics, the cascading feedback loops, and the systemic risk propagation. Whether any layer provides the operational capacity to detect them depends on capabilities none of these vendors were built to deliver.

The test is straightforward: does this investment make the institution harder to break, faster to recover, and more capable of noticing when something is wrong? Or does it make someone else's quarterly numbers while the institution's actual exposure persists behind a more expensive facade? In financial services, the facade is more expensive than anywhere else, because the compliance culture is deeper, the budgets are larger, and the distance between the purchased assurance and the actual risk has never been wider.

The signature still means nothing. It just costs more now. Why wouldn't it? Assurance is a product, and the market sets the price.

# Chapter 18: The Cascade Already Underway

Competitive pressure ensures you will pursue AI convergence regardless of risks documented in this analysis. Your question is not whether to adopt, but whether to adopt thoughtfully or recklessly.

Every control has a failure mode. You survive by understanding what happens when your controls fail, and building for that understanding.

Board-level AI committees should include directors with genuine AI expertise who can challenge management, not approve presentations. Executive accountability must be explicit: someone must own AI risk, with compensation tied to that responsibility. This is the theory. The practice is that boards approve what they do not understand, because the alternative is admitting they cannot govern what they oversee. The executive who "owns" AI risk owns a system they cannot audit, built on mathematics they cannot interpret, operating at speeds they cannot perceive. When this governance fails and the board-approved system causes harm, the failure is structural, not personal. The accountability framework assumes understanding that does not exist. The signature on the approval document means nothing. Everyone knows. The document exists for regulators who need someone to hold responsible.

Pre-trade controls establish boundaries AI systems cannot exceed: position limits, loss thresholds, volatility triggers. When these fail and conditions exceed the boundaries' calibration, the AI continues operating in territory the controls were designed to prevent. Boundaries set for normal conditions prove inadequate for unusual conditions. The extreme scenarios where human judgment matters most are the scenarios where pre-trade controls provide least protection.

Kill switches provide emergency shutdown when AI behavior becomes problematic. When these fail, when unusual activity takes too long to become observable, too long to be assessed as problematic, too long to escalate to someone with authority, substantial damage occurs before the switch is pulled. Kill switches limit cascading failures. They do not prevent initial failures. By the time you reach for the switch, the cascade is already underway.

Real-time monitoring uses AI to watch AI, detecting anomalies and alerting operators. When the monitoring AI shares blind spots with the trading AI, both having learned from similar data, novel failure modes are not recognized. The monitoring system confidently reports that nothing is wrong while something unprecedented unfolds. And even when monitoring works perfectly, escalation still requires human action at human speeds in a system operating at machine speeds.

Graceful degradation allows operations to continue when AI fails. When this fails, when the fallback procedures were not tested recently, when the humans who should execute them have skills atrophied from disuse, when the communication protocols break down under stress, the institution discovers that "graceful" degradation requires capabilities it no longer possesses. The skill atrophy compounds the problem. Human capability preservation requires intentional maintenance: exercises without AI assistance, training that keeps manual skills sharp. This has costs that compete with efficiency gains. Most institutions underinvest. They discover the underinvestment when AI failure during market stress coincides with conditions where human judgment is most needed and least available.

Model lifecycle management ensures documented ownership, validation, and retirement criteria throughout operational life. This fails when models remain in production past their validated conditions, when ownership transfers without knowledge transfer, when retirement criteria are waived for business reasons; the institution then operates with AI that no one fully understands and no one can entirely justify. The documentation exists. It no longer reflects reality.

Automated containment responds faster than humans can, taking protective action while humans assess situations. When this fails, when the containment logic itself contains errors, when the protective actions trigger unintended consequences, when the automated response is worse than the problem it addresses, the institution has outsourced judgment to systems that cannot exercise it.

The human role has shifted from decision-maker to governor and auditor. But governors cannot govern what they cannot perceive. Auditors cannot audit what they cannot understand.

These controls are not worthless. They are inadequate.

The distinction matters. Inadequate controls, understood as inadequate, provide some protection while maintaining appropriate humility. Inadequate controls, believed to be sufficient, provide false confidence that makes failures worse when they arrive.

You cannot build systems that do not fail. You can build systems that fail less catastrophically. You can build an organization that learns from failures rather than concealing them. You can build a culture that treats every incident as information rather than embarrassment. The institutions that share incident lessons build collective resilience. The institutions that conceal incidents contribute to industry vulnerability, including their own.

No one has solved these problems. If you acknowledge the unsolved nature of the problems, you are better positioned than those who believe their current controls are correct. They are the best anyone has managed so far. And the best anyone has managed so far may not be enough.

We are building systems whose behavior we cannot fully predict, deploying them at speeds that exceed human oversight capacity, in interconnected environments where individual failures cascade systemically. Financial services is the sector most transformed by AI convergence because it is, at its core, information processing. Healthcare involves human bodies. Critical infrastructure involves physical systems. Financial services involves data and the decisions made on that data. When AI processes data and makes decisions faster than humans, and it does, the transformation is total. The efficiency gains come bundled with the vulnerabilities. They are the same feature, viewed from different angles.

The milliseconds matter. So does the wisdom to know what speed cannot provide.

*When You're Not the Systemically Important Bank*

The scenarios in this part describe global systemically important banks, high-frequency trading operations, institutions with model risk management teams and dedicated AI governance functions. The Flash Crash happened on trading floors most financial professionals will never see. The millisecond operations outpacing human oversight occur in systems most institutions will never build.

Most financial services operates at a different scale and a different speed.

The community bank with $800 million in assets serves a regional market with a technology team that also manages the branch network, the ATMs, and the phone system. The credit union with 40,000 members adopted AI-powered fraud detection because its core banking vendor included it in the latest platform upgrade. The regional insurance company uses AI underwriting tools selected by a consulting firm that no longer supports the implementation. The independent financial advisor relies on AI-driven portfolio analytics from a platform whose model methodology is proprietary and undisclosed.

These organizations do not operate at millisecond speed. They do not face Flash Crash dynamics. But they face every other convergence risk described in this part, and several that hit harder at smaller scale.

The vendor dependency is more complete. A global bank can negotiate model transparency requirements, demand validation access, maintain internal teams capable of independent model assessment. A community bank accepts the fraud detection model its core provider ships.

It cannot audit the model. It cannot validate the training data. It cannot assess whether the model performs differently for the demographics its community actually serves versus the national dataset it was trained on. Models drift; when this one does, the community bank learns through denied transactions that should have been approved and approved transactions that should have been denied. The feedback arrives as customer complaints, not model monitoring.

The regulatory exposure is disproportionate. SR 11-7, the Federal Reserve's model risk management guidance, applies to institutions of all sizes. The expectations for model validation, ongoing monitoring, and governance documentation do not scale with the institution's resources. A community bank examined on its AI model governance faces the same conceptual requirements as a global bank, with a fraction of the expertise to satisfy them. The compliance burden falls equally. The capacity to bear it does not.

The accountability diffusion described in Chapter 15 becomes more acute. The AI-driven lending model produces disparate outcomes: it approves loans at different rates for different demographics. The global bank has fair lending analysts who might detect the pattern. The community bank has a compliance officer who also handles BSA/AML, Community Reinvestment Act (CRA), and consumer complaints. The pattern may persist for years, creating legal exposure that accumulates silently until an examination or a lawsuit surfaces it.

Resource-constrained financial institutions share the strategic framework from the prior book: concentrate vendor relationships, document AI-influenced decisions, maintain exit plans. For financial services specifically, three additional principles apply.

First, treat every AI-influenced lending, underwriting, and account decision as a fair lending decision, because regulators will. Document the human review that occurred. Record when officers override AI recommendations and why. This documentation is not bureaucratic overhead. It is the institution's evidence that it exercised judgment rather than outsourcing it to a model it cannot explain.

Second, demand that core banking and technology vendors provide model performance data disaggregated by the demographics the institution actually serves. A fraud model trained nationally may perform differently in a community where transaction patterns reflect local economic characteristics. The institution cannot validate what the vendor will not disclose. But it can track false positive rates by customer segment, approval rates by demographic category, and error patterns by product type, then use that operational data to identify where vendor models may be failing its specific market.

Third, use the existing collaborative infrastructure. The infrastructure for collective action already exists: community bank consortiums, credit union service organizations, state banking associations, groups like the ICBA and CUNA. These provide channels for sharing AI implementation experiences, pooling vendor evaluation resources, and collectively negotiating transparency requirements no individual small institution could demand. The community bank that discovers its fraud model flags immigrant remittance patterns at disproportionate rates needs a mechanism to determine whether the problem is local or systemic. Without collective channels, each institution discovers the same failure independently.

*Paying for Patterns That Don't Fit*

The fraud model flags the transaction. Again.

Elena Vasquez has owned a commercial cleaning business for eleven years. Twice a month, for seven years, she has wired the same approximate amount to the same supplier in Monterrey for industrial cleaning chemicals. The relationship predates the bank's AI upgrade.

Since the upgrade, one in three of her wire transfers triggers a fraud alert. The transaction freezes. Her business account locks. She calls the branch. The branch manager, who has known Elena since she opened the account, calls the fraud department. The fraud department reviews the alert, finds nothing wrong, releases the funds. Elapsed time: four to six hours. Her supplier holds the shipment. Her crews arrive at buildings without the materials to clean them.

The bank cannot explain why the model flags Elena's transactions. The model cannot explain either. What it learned, trained on transaction patterns across a national dataset, is that wire transfers to Mexico with certain characteristics correlate with fraud risk. Elena's transactions match those characteristics. That the characteristics reflect legitimate commerce in border communities, that the "fraud signal" is actually a demographic signal, that Elena has never committed fraud and never will. None of this appears in the training data in ways the model can distinguish.

Elena is not a false positive. She is a true negative the model cannot recognize.

The fraud department sees individual cases. Elena calls, the alert clears, the transaction processes. Resolved. But Elena is not alone. The Ethiopian restaurant owner whose supplier payments to Addis Ababa freeze. The Filipino nurse sending remittances to Manila through patterns the model learned to distrust. The halal grocery whose cash deposit frequency triggers structuring alerts designed for money launderers.

Each case resolves individually. The pattern never surfaces.

The model optimizes for fraud prevention. It succeeds. Fraud losses decline. The cost distributes unevenly. Customers whose transaction patterns match the training data's conception of "normal" experience seamless service. For customers whose communities, commerce, and family obligations cross borders the training data treated as risk factors, that deviation produces friction that accumulates into something heavier.

The compliance officer reviewing Elena's fifth escalation cannot audit what the model saw. She can document the override. She cannot fix the pattern. The vendor does not disaggregate false positive rates by customer demographics. The community bank lacks the statistical capacity to perform that analysis itself. It knows Elena. It does not know how many Elenas it doesn't know: customers who closed their accounts rather than endure another frozen transaction, who experienced the friction as rejection and left.

The model's aggregate performance metrics look excellent. The harm hides in the residuals.

The millisecond dynamics that dominate this part's analysis do not apply to most financial institutions. The convergence dynamics do. The community bank's AI risk is not a Flash Crash. It is the slow accumulation of model-driven decisions that no one in the institution fully understands, producing outcomes that no one monitors with sufficient granularity, creating exposure that surfaces only when the cost of discovery exceeds the cost of prevention. The speed is different. The trajectory is the same.

*What This Reveals*

Time collapses differently here. The grid operator has seconds. The physician has minutes. The trader has already lost.

This is what the preceding chapters expose: financial services operates beyond the horizon of human intervention. Not as a failure of governance, but as a mathematical fact. The cascade that begins at 09:31:04.003 has executed thousands of trades before the first human sees an alert. The signature on the approval document, the one the head of algorithmic trading described as "a legal fiction that everyone pretends is meaningful oversight" is not negligence. It is the only option available when the systems move faster than neurons can fire.

And yet the accountability frameworks, the regulatory requirements, the governance structures all assume someone is deciding. Someone is responsible. Someone could have intervened.

The fiction persists because the alternative is admitting what this part has documented: that we have built systems whose failure modes outpace our capacity to prevent them, whose consequences propagate through interconnections we cannot fully map, whose correlated behaviors emerge from training on the same data in ways no individual institution can see. The Flash Crash was a preview. The AI systems operating today are faster, more sophisticated, more deeply integrated. The recovery may not be as quick.

What financial services reveals is not a sector-specific problem. It is the limit case of what happens when AI convergence reaches systems where the human intervention window approaches zero. Healthcare is traveling toward that limit. Critical infrastructure is closer than it knows. Financial services has already arrived, and is sending back reports from the other side.

# Part V : Cross-Sector Synthesis

## Chapter 19: The Fault Line Beneath

The tensions do not resolve.

Efficiency against resilience. Innovation against caution. Automation against human judgment. These are not problems awaiting solutions. They are permanent features of a transformation with no stable endpoint, navigable only by organizations that understand what they are navigating. Some challenges have no good answers. What follows does not pretend otherwise.

But the challenges share a geometry worth understanding before anything else.

By now you have seen this geometry sector by sector. The Purdue model's hierarchy becomes a mesh. Inference attacks reconstructing what patients chose to hide. Cross-product correlations exposing institutions to violations across twelve jurisdictions simultaneously. The mechanisms differ. The dynamic is identical: boundaries that once contained information no longer hold when AI synthesizes across them. These are not parallel problems requiring parallel solutions. They are the same problem, compounding wherever the sectors connect.

The terrain exists whether you have mapped it or not. Adversaries are already learning to navigate it.

*The Errors the Landscape Generates*

AI hallucination, the generation of plausible but incorrect information with inappropriate confidence, is not a bug to be fixed. It is a mathematical property of how large language models represent knowledge. What varies is consequence: a hallucinated contract clause causes different damage than a hallucinated cancer diagnosis or a hallucinated trading signal. The defense mechanisms are conceptually identical. Their calibration must reflect sector-specific stakes.

Prompt injection, model poisoning, adversarial examples, supply chain attacks: these are not sector-specific vulnerabilities. They are properties of how AI systems process inputs, learn from data, and depend on external components. The attack surfaces differ. The mathematics are the same.

Where the mathematics diverge is in consequence, which is measured in coupling.

*Three Distances from Irreversibility*

Critical infrastructure occupies one end of the spectrum. AI systems controlling power grids, water treatment, or transportation do not just process information, they actuate physical systems. A compromised AI opens valves, closes switches, reroutes trains. The time between AI decision and physical consequence is measured in seconds or less. Graceful degradation requirements in this sector are not aspirational. They are operational necessities validated by every blackout and system failure. But AI's probabilistic behaviors do not map cleanly to the deterministic safety systems those principles assume. The tension remains unresolved.

Healthcare occupies the middle. Human clinicians typically intervene between AI output and patient outcome, a buffer that previous chapters documented in detail and showed to be eroding visit by visit. The human buffer only works if humans understand when they are receiving AI-influenced information and can exercise independent judgment. Opacity undermines this buffer even when the AI performs correctly.

Financial services operates with the loosest physical coupling but the highest systemic interdependence. AI decisions move money, not molecules. A trading algorithm's error does not physically harm anyone in the immediate moment. But financial systems' interconnections mean that errors propagate through markets, institutions, and ultimately economies in ways that other sectors' errors do not. The 2010 Flash Crash demonstrated this propagation at algorithm speeds: a 1,000-point Dow drop in minutes. The recovery was similarly rapid; markets rebounded within hours. Physical systems cannot recover so quickly. A collapsed bridge stays collapsed. Financial systems' loose physical coupling enables both faster failures and faster recoveries.

*The Oversight That Remains*

Human oversight requirements vary. Critical infrastructure's seconds-level response times confine human oversight to system design and parameter setting, never real-time decision review. Healthcare's minutes-to-hours decision timescales allow human review for high-stakes decisions. For now. Financial services' microsecond operations eliminate human review for individual transactions, concentrating human judgment on strategy and system monitoring.

Recovery complexity also varies. Physical systems damaged by AI errors require physical repair. Healthcare harm to individual patients may be permanent even when the AI error is corrected. Financial systems can often undo an erroneous transaction even when its systemic effects prove permanent.

Three sectors. One geometry. Three different distances between error and irreversibility. Same cliff, different drop.

The systems that carry these sectors forward were not built for this moment. They were built decades ago, by people who understood them completely, and many of those people are gone.

# Chapter 20: What Keeps Me Awake

Every sector carries technical debt, and the debts differ: five decades of SCADA protocols in critical infrastructure, fragmented EHR architectures in healthcare, COBOL foundations in financial services. But the dynamic is identical. AI convergence must accommodate systems designed for different assumptions about connectivity, security, and operational tempo.

These systems are load-bearing walls. Society's essential functions run on this infrastructure today.

March 2024, Regional Medical Center. 02:14:07 EST. The AI clinical decision support system, integrated six months prior with the legacy EHR, begins correlating emergency department presentations. Pattern recognition triggers sepsis alerts for twelve patients simultaneously. The alerts route correctly through the modern interface, but the underlying EHR, built in 2003, lacks capacity for concurrent alert processing. By 02:14:23, the queue backs up. The most critical alert, for a 67-year-old in early septic shock, arrives four and a half minutes after generation. The AI performed exactly as designed. So did the legacy system. The failure existed in the space between them.

Familiar systems carry known risks. AI-enhanced replacements carry unknown ones. Their behavior is less well understood. In the short term, replacement may actually increase operational risk. The utility, hospital, or bank that moves slowly is not necessarily behind. It may be appropriately cautious given what it has to lose.

"The executives want me to explain why we can't just upgrade," observes a systems architect at a major health system. "They show me vendors promising seamless integration. I show them the 847 custom interfaces we've built over twenty years. They say we need to modernize. I say: what happens to the patients when we're halfway through modernization and the old system is half-dismantled and the new system isn't yet reliable? They don't have an answer. I don't either. But I know which question keeps me awake."

Legacy systems share another vulnerability: inadequate documentation. The engineers who built them have retired or died. AI systems learn from the data they receive, including patterns created by undocumented workarounds and historical accidents no one remembers. An AI optimizing operations might learn to avoid certain sequences without anyone understanding those sequences were prohibited because of an incident decades ago. AI systems cannot learn what has never been recorded.

And the people who might have filled those gaps are disappearing.

The pace of workforce displacement varies. Critical infrastructure experiences the slowest: operational roles require physical presence and judgment AI augments rather than replaces. Financial services experiences the fastest: the sector is information processing. Healthcare occupies the middle, with administrative functions highly vulnerable while clinical roles retain the human connection patients value.

Each sector faces a distinct insider threat profile. Critical infrastructure focuses on traditional insider threat management.

Healthcare confronts professionals under competitive pressure from AI. Financial services faces displacement-driven insider threat at scale, as workers with intimate system knowledge face role elimination.

But across all three sectors, the same paradox tightens.

AI systems require human oversight. Reliance on AI degrades the human skills that make oversight meaningful. The physician who has relied on AI diagnostic support may find, when AI fails, that their own clinical judgment has degraded. The grid operator who trusted AI optimization may struggle to manage operations manually during an outage.

November 2025, Trading Floor, Chicago. 09:42:17 CST. The quantitative model produces an output flagged as anomalous. The human trader has never overridden the model in three years. It has been right. Now she stares at the flag. The model says hold. The oversight system says the model may be wrong. Her own instinct, atrophied from disuse, says nothing useful. She calls her supervisor. He has never overridden the model either. They escalate. By the time someone with authority makes a decision, the window has closed. Later analysis suggests a novel failure mode. Later analysis cannot tell them what the right answer would have been.

AI failures correlate with crisis conditions, exactly when human skills matter most. The healthcare AI trained on normal presentations fails during pandemics. The grid AI trained on typical patterns fails during extreme weather. The humans who must take over are those whose skills have been least exercised.

The universal response is intentional preservation of human capability through exercises without AI assistance. These exercises compete with efficiency gains, yet without them AI failure becomes organizational paralysis. The tension cannot be fully resolved. All organizations navigate a tradeoff with no optimal point.

Organizational culture shapes how that tradeoff plays out. Critical infrastructure's safety culture provides natural resistance to unsafe AI recommendations. Healthcare's physician autonomy can either provide human checks or create shadow workflows that bypass controls. Financial services' performance culture drives rapid AI adoption but also security shortcuts when controls are perceived as friction.

Meanwhile, the skills gap widens into something more dangerous than a staffing problem. AI convergence demands expertise that does not exist in sufficient quantity: OT engineers who understand AI in critical infrastructure, clinical informaticists who understand AI security in healthcare, quantitative analysts who understand AI vulnerabilities in financial services. Training takes years. The deployment timeline does not wait. This creates a divide between those who understand AI systems and those who must work alongside them without that understanding. A grid operator who cannot interpret AI recommendations. A nurse who cannot evaluate algorithmic alerts. A trader who cannot question model outputs. These workers face a choice between blind trust and reflexive rejection. Neither is adequate.

And the adversaries are not waiting either. Critical infrastructure faces the most concentrated nation-state threat: Russia, China, Iran, North Korea bring different capabilities but all target power grids, water systems, and transportation networks as strategic assets. Healthcare faces threats for pharmaceutical research and pandemic response intelligence. Financial services faces threats for sanctions evasion and market manipulation. AI convergence creates new opportunities for all of them. Systems synthesizing data across previously isolated environments create single points of compromise. Model poisoning enables systematic manipulation that might not manifest until a crisis, the moment when the poisoned output matters most.

Across all sectors, the contest between AI-powered attack and defense has no stable equilibrium. Asymmetric costs favor attackers. Defenders must protect all vectors while attackers need find only one. Capability democratization puts sophisticated tools within reach of unsophisticated actors. Organizations cannot expect to win permanently. The realistic objective is making attacks expensive enough to deter many adversaries and contain losses from those who persist.

Communities served by critical infrastructure, patients in healthcare systems, and depositors in financial institutions all depend on organizations managing AI competently. When skills gaps leave organizations unable to govern their AI systems, consequences reach everyone those organizations serve. The skills gap is not an operational problem. It is a vector through which institutional failure becomes societal harm.

# Chapter 21: Every Component Worked

When information systems evolve faster than governance frameworks, failures become inevitable. Enron's executives exploited complexity to hide reality from investors, regulators, and their own board. AI convergence creates analogous complexity. These systems synthesize, obscure, and generate information in ways dwarfing Enron-era capability.

The regulatory responses to Enron created governance requirements that reshaped corporate accountability. AI convergence is producing analogous responses. Organizations that build governance capacity before requirements arrive will shape those requirements. Those that wait will be shaped by them.

But the frameworks meant to govern these systems were not designed for what AI has become. NERC CIP assumes deterministic systems. HIPAA assumes specific data flows. Securities and Exchange Commission regulations assume decisions can be explained. AI convergence violates every one of these assumptions while creating governance gaps no existing framework addresses.

The result is accountability diffused to the point of meaninglessness. When AI systems contribute to decisions causing harm, the chain of responsibility dissolves. The model was developed by vendors, trained on unaudited data, making recommendations through processes the organization does not understand, followed by humans who may or may not have exercised independent judgment.

"I have sign-off authority for a system I cannot audit, built by a vendor who will not explain it," observes a chief risk officer at a regional bank. "Every lawyer tells me accountability is clear: it's mine. Every technologist tells me the system is fine: trust the model. I sign approvals because my job requires it. Whether I am actually providing oversight or merely a signature for legal purposes, I genuinely do not know."

In healthcare, the diffusion affects malpractice liability. In financial services, regulatory compliance. In critical infrastructure, safety investigations. Explicit accountability assignments must come before AI deployment, not after it.

And the sectors do not operate in isolation.

Healthcare and financial services depend on critical infrastructure. Hospitals cannot operate without power. Financial transactions require telecommunications. An AI-related failure in the power grid affects every hospital whose backup power eventually depletes and every financial institution whose trading systems go dark.

August 2025, Midwest Regional Grid. 15:47:22 CDT. The AI load-balancing system misinterprets data from a compromised sensor network, its trusted sensors reached by opportunistic criminal access. For eleven minutes, the AI redistributes load based on phantom demand. At 15:58:14, the first hospital switches to backup generators. By 16:12:33, seventeen hospitals are on backup. Two surgical suites abort procedures. One trading floor loses connectivity for twenty-three minutes. The root cause report notes that every component worked. The system failed.

Healthcare and financial services intertwine through insurance, billing, and investment relationships. The separation between sectors that regulatory frameworks assume does not match the integrated reality AI convergence creates. Cross-sector interdependencies demand security architectures acknowledging external dependencies. Information sharing across sectors becomes security necessity, not compliance checkbox. No individual utility, hospital, or bank can secure interdependent systems alone.

These interdependencies surface questions no one has answered. How should organizations balance efficiency against security when no methodology quantifies either with confidence? How should displaced workers maintain livelihoods when required skills cannot be acquired faster than roles disappear? How should regulators govern systems evolving faster than regulatory cycles? How should societies ensure accountability when AI diffuses responsibility across vendors, operators, and the mathematical properties of models themselves?

This book does not pretend to have answers. What it has is a mapping of territory, an honest assessment that traces where pressures converge, where tensions remain unresolved, and where consequences extend beyond organizational boundaries.

What the sectors have learned, separately, deserves hearing together. Critical infrastructure knows that systems which cannot tolerate downtime require defensive depth AI enthusiasm often underestimates. The graceful degradation requirements developed over decades apply because they work: fail-safe mechanisms, defense in depth, preserved manual capabilities. Healthcare knows that AI decisions affecting individual humans carry ethical weight pure optimization cannot capture. The consent paradoxes, bias implications, and irreducible need for human judgment are dimensions efficiency metrics alone cannot address. Financial services knows that speed creates vulnerability as surely as capability. The millisecond operations outpacing human oversight, systemic interdependencies propagating failures faster than anyone responds, arms race dynamics with no stable equilibrium, velocity is not inherently virtuous.

Beneath these lessons lies a deeper fracture. Legacy systems are not merely technical constraints; they are infrastructure on which modern life depends. The power grid controls built decades ago still deliver electricity. The COBOL programs still process transactions constituting the economy. These systems cannot be wished away. AI convergence that ignores this reality creates fragility. Organizations prioritizing AI capability over integration stability risk failures affecting everyone who depends on them.

The human skillset divide threatens something more profound than technological disruption alone. When workers cannot understand AI systems alongside which they work, they lose not just job security but professional identity and meaningful participation in their labor. The grid operator who cannot interpret AI outputs. The nurse who cannot evaluate algorithmic recommendations. The analyst whose judgment has atrophied. These are human beings whose expertise is becoming illegible to systems mediating their work. Organizations failing to invest in human capability development abandon the people whose competence their operations require.

If these concerns remain unacknowledged, consequences will not be confined to quarterly reports. Patients will receive care from systems no one in the room fully understands. Power will flow through grids managed by algorithms operators accept without comprehension. Workers who once possessed operational knowledge will have been displaced or deskilled, leaving no one capable of intervening when AI is wrong. This is not a speculative future. It is a trajectory already in motion.

When lights go out, people suffer and die. When diagnoses are wrong, patients are harmed. When markets fail, economies contract and livelihoods disappear. The Texas grid failure of 2021 was not an AI failure, but showed what happens when infrastructure fails at scale. The Flash Crash of 2010 demonstrated how quickly algorithmic failures cascade. As AI convergence proceeds, the potential for AI-related contributions to such events grows.

Organizations and regulators cannot afford to learn through catastrophic experience.

# Chapter 22: The Gold Rush

The Preface named it. The sector chapters showed it. Now see it whole.

Every major transformation in information technology has spawned industries dedicated to managing its consequences. The filing cabinet created records management. The database created the compliance industry: armies of auditors, tool vendors, and consultants who profit from the complexity they help organizations navigate. Each wave generated genuine value alongside genuine exploitation, and the two were rarely easy to distinguish in real time.

AI convergence is following the same pattern. The risks documented in this book are real. The market assembling around those risks is also real, and it does not always share your interests.

*The AI Convergence Trap* identified this dynamic in general terms and called it the AI Security-Commercial Complex: the ecosystem of vendors, consultants, and platform providers whose business models depend on the persistence of the problems they claim to solve. The sector chapters showed what it looks like in practice. It is worth seeing those practices side by side, because the pattern sharpens when the sectors are viewed together.

*Three Sectors, One Playbook*

The preceding chapters documented the pattern in sector-specific detail: the OT vendor rebranding protocol analyzers as "AI-aware monitoring" while missing adversarial inputs entirely. The Big

Four repackaging GRC as "AI governance advisory" while the signature on the approval document remains a legal fiction. The HIPAA compliance platform generating documentation that satisfies auditors evaluating controls that predate the threat. The physician becoming the de facto quality assurance layer for diagnostic AI whose validation methodology she was never shown.

The structure is identical across all three: genuine capability wrapped in overstated coverage, sold to buyers who lack the expertise to distinguish the two. You're not buying security. You're buying the feeling of security. And the invoice looks the same either way.

But the pattern reveals more than repetition when the examples are placed side by side with the same lens applied to each.

The utility purchased "AI-aware OT monitoring." What did it think it bought? Coverage for its AI-driven load forecasting system, the same one Chapter 5 showed could be manipulated through corrupted weather data. What did it actually get? A protocol analyzer that still detects anomalous Modbus and DNP3 traffic, the same capability it had before the rebrand. What remains exposed? Everything Chapter 8's auditor couldn't find a checkbox for: adversarial inputs crafted to exploit the forecasting model, training data poisoning in sensor feeds, optimization drift converging toward harm. The tool monitors the pipes. The threat lives in the predictions flowing through them.

The hospital's EHR vendor activated AI diagnostic features by default in a platform update. Then it began selling governance tools to manage the features it had switched on without asking. What did the hospital think it bought? Oversight of its AI deployment. What did it actually get? The vendor governing itself, through a product that generates the documentation accreditors will want to see. What remains exposed? The 94% confidence hallucination from Chapter 10: the pancreatic cancer that didn't exist, the unnecessary surgery, the patient whose trust never recovered. The governance tool tracks whether the feature is enabled and who can access it. It does not track whether the feature is *right*.

The bank engaged a Big Four firm for AI governance advisory. The partners know what examiners want to see. They built careers navigating Sarbanes-Oxley and Basel III. What did the bank think it bought? A framework ensuring its AI lending models comply with fair lending requirements. What did it actually get? A mapping of AI operations to existing regulatory expectations: thorough, professionally delivered, and silent on every risk that falls outside those expectations. What remains exposed? The fiction Chapter 17 documented: post-hoc explanations generated to satisfy adverse action requirements, explanations the chief compliance officer openly acknowledged bear uncertain resemblance to what the AI actually did. The framework governs the documentation. The model governs the decisions. The gap between them is where the risk lives.

Three vendors. Three buyers. Three invoices paid in full. In every case, the buyer received genuine capability: real monitoring, real documentation, real regulatory mapping. In every case, the capability stopped where the AI-specific risk began. And in every case, the buyer lacked the expertise to see the gap.

What makes the gap so hard to see is that the people across the table are not charlatans. The presentations are technically literate. The whitepapers cite real research. The teams include genuine data scientists, credentialed engineers, and PhDs who understand the mathematics better than you do. That expertise is real and it is what makes the overstated coverage invisible.

A mediocre vendor is easy to dismiss. A brilliant one who wraps genuine capability in a narrative of comprehensive protection is almost impossible to challenge without matching expertise you probably don't have and they know you don't have. The sophistication is not the antidote to the gap. It is the camouflage.

*The Distinguishing Question*

The commercial complex is not uniformly harmful. Some vendors deliver genuine resilience. Some consultants understand the territory well enough to guide organizations through it honestly. The problem isn't that the market exists but that it rewards the appearance of security as readily as its substance, and the buyer often cannot tell the difference.

One question separates genuine investment from purchased confidence: Does this make us harder to break, faster to recover, and more capable of noticing when something is wrong? Or does it make someone else's quarterly numbers while our actual exposure persists behind a more expensive facade?

Consider what happens when someone actually asks it.

A regional utility, after reading a draft version of this book's critical infrastructure chapters, ran an adversarial exercise against its newly purchased AI monitoring platform. The red team fed subtly corrupted weather data into the load forecasting model, not random noise but the kind of systematic bias Chapter 5 described, the kind a patient adversary would craft. The monitoring platform reported nothing. It was watching network traffic for protocol anomalies. The attack lived in the data, not the protocol. The forecasting model adjusted its predictions. The dispatch decisions shifted. The monitoring dashboard remained green. The utility had spent seven figures on a tool that would have watched the grid degrade and reported that everything was fine.

A mid-sized health system asked its EHR vendor a version of the same question: can your governance module detect when the diagnostic AI produces a high-confidence hallucination? The vendor's response was revealing: the module tracks model versioning, user access, and feature utilization. It logs which clinicians interact with AI outputs and whether they accept or override recommendations. It does not evaluate whether the recommendations are clinically sound. That, the vendor explained, remains the clinician's responsibility. The system that was sold as governance turned out to be an activity log. The physician with eleven minutes is still the last line of defense, and no one has told her that the governance tools her hospital purchased were never designed to help.

Ask it of every vendor, every platform, every consulting engagement, every governance framework. It must be asked by someone with enough technical understanding to evaluate the answer, which returns us to the skills gap this book has documented across every sector. Organizations that lack the internal expertise to evaluate vendor claims become dependent on vendors to evaluate themselves. The conflict of interest is structural and unresolvable through contract terms alone.

Boards that approve AI security budgets without the literacy to evaluate what those budgets purchase are not exercising oversight. They are purchasing the appearance of oversight, the same dynamic *The AI Convergence Trap* documented in its chapter on board accountability, now multiplied across sectors where the consequences of illusory governance include blackouts, misdiagnoses, and market failures.

The gold rush is underway. The prospectors are selling picks and shovels. Some of the picks work. Some are painted wood.

You must learn to tell the difference because no one selling picks has any incentive to teach you.

*What This Reveals*

The sectors don't run parallel; they carry each other's weight.

The grid powers the hospital. The hospital's billing feeds the insurer. The insurer's liquidity positions flow through trading systems that price risk based on assumptions about grid reliability and healthcare costs. When one fails, the failure does not stay local. It propagates through connections that no organizational chart depicts, no regulatory framework governs, no governance committee has mapped. The cascade that begins with corrupted sensor data at a regional utility arrives at a trading floor in Chicago before anyone has identified the origin. The diagnostic AI that hallucinates in a rural clinic creates billing anomalies that ripple through a reinsurance model that adjusts risk pricing that influences grid investment that shapes the reliability the hospital was depending on.

This is what the cross-sector synthesis reveals: the geometry of fragility is three-dimensional. The six risk primitives (dissolved boundaries, inference exposure, instruction compromise, error propagation, vendor opacity, speed as force multiplier) do not operate independently in each sector. They compound across sectors. The same prompt injection technique targets the utility, the hospital, and the bank. The same training data gaps affect models deployed in all three. The same vendor supplies AI components to systems that depend on each other without knowing they depend on each other.

No single sector can secure itself. The utility that builds perfect resilience remains vulnerable to cascades originating in healthcare systems it does not control. The hospital that governs its AI flawlessly inherits risk from grid failures it cannot prevent. The bank that monitors its models continuously depends on infrastructure whose AI it cannot audit. The only adequate response is one no governance framework yet supports: coordination across sectors that have never coordinated, visibility into dependencies that have never been mapped, and humility about a system of systems whose failure modes we are only beginning to understand.

The gold rush will not teach you this. The vendors selling picks have no incentive to explain that the mountain they are helping you mine sits atop a fault line that runs through every sector at once. That knowledge falls to you, and to the recognition that what any one organization builds is only as resilient as the weakest system it depends on.

# Epilogue: Every Tuesday

You have now seen what Tuesday looks like from the inside.

This journey has not solved the problems it documents, and it has not pretended to. The tensions between efficiency and resilience, between automation and human judgment, between speed and oversight: these tensions do not resolve. They persist as permanent features of a future transformation with no stable endpoint. Organizations that pretend otherwise build systems that will fail in predictable ways. Those that acknowledge these tensions and build adaptable systems with awareness of their imperfections will succeed.

The difference is not academic. It is the difference between the utility that survived the coordinated attack and the one that didn't. The survivor didn't predict the specific threat; it preserved the capacity to respond when prediction failed.

The questions that remain are not comfortable. How do you govern systems you cannot audit, built on mathematics you cannot interpret, operating at speeds you cannot perceive? How do you maintain human judgment as a vital capability when every incentive rewards replacing it? How do you prepare for failure modes that emerge only under the crisis conditions where preparation matters most and practice has been least? How do you secure systems whose behavior you are still discovering, against adversaries learning the attack surface at the same pace you are, under governance frameworks that assume a world that no longer exists?

These are not problems you solve. They are conditions you inherit.

And these conditions do not require full convergence to matter. The dynamics documented here are already present in every AI deployment, however partial: dissolved boundaries, hallucination under automation bias, vendor opacity, expertise erosion, the compliance mirage. The hospital using a single diagnostic model faces the same trust calibration problem as the converged system. The utility piloting predictive maintenance inherits the same vendor dependency. The bank deploying fraud detection confronts the same explainability gap. Full convergence amplifies these risks without creating them. If you are deploying AI at all, even today, you are already inside this book.

The instinct will be to treat this as a catalog of fears: to file the risks, staff the committees, check the boxes, and move on. That instinct is the compliance mirage this book has documented across every sector. The signature on the approval document that means nothing. The governance that exists for documentation purposes. The review that provides legal cover without ensuring review actually occurred.

Do not trust that instinct. It will cost you everything.

Fortunately, the AI Security–Commercial Complex described in the previous chapter will be the first to show up at your door, armed with solutions, confident answers, and promises to put leadership at ease. But before you let them in, pause and ask the one question that matters.

Because what no vendor can sell you is the thing that actually stands between your organization and catastrophe. No platform can automate it, no consultant can deliver it, no governance framework can mandate it into existence, regardless of cost or time. It is you.

The humans you remove during convergence look like overhead. They are the last redundancy.

They are the only systems capable of recognizing what AI cannot: that the answer doesn't match the context, that the recommendation makes no sense given what happened last quarter, that the confidence score is high but the conclusion is wrong.

Remove them, and you have optimized away your margin for error when your exposure to error has never been greater.

Preserve them, and you have something no algorithm provides: judgment under uncertainty, the capacity to doubt what the system insists is true, the willingness to pull the switch before the cascade reaches the next domino.

The convergence is not coming. It is here. The dominoes are already in motion.

*Life finds a way. So does chaos. So does AI.*

The last redundancy isn't a system. It's a choice—yours, made fresh every day you show up and refuse to trust what you cannot verify.

# References and Further Reading for the Sector-Specific Supplement

## Critical Infrastructure Security & Incidents

Cybersecurity and Infrastructure Security Agency and Federal Bureau of Investigation. *DarkSide Ransomware: Best Practices for Preventing Business Disruption from Ransomware Attacks (AA21-131A).* CISA, 2021.

Cybersecurity and Infrastructure Security Agency, Federal Bureau of Investigation, Environmental Protection Agency, and Multi-State Information Sharing and Analysis Center. *Compromise of U.S. Water Treatment Facility (AA21-042A).*CISA, 2021.

Dragos, Inc. *CRASHOVERRIDE: Analysis of the Threat to Electric Grid Operations.* Dragos, Inc., 2017.

E-ISAC and SANS ICS. *Analysis of the Cyber Attack on the Ukrainian Power Grid.* Electricity Information Sharing and Analysis Center, 2016.

Greenberg, Andy. *Sandworm: A New Era of Cyberwar and the Hunt for the Kremlin's Most Dangerous Hackers.* Doubleday, 2019.

King, Douglas E., and Michael J. Assante. "The Industrial Control System (ICS) Cyber Kill Chain." *SANS Institute,* 2015.

North American Electric Reliability Corporation. *CIP Standards.* NERC, 2023.

Texas Comptroller of Public Accounts. *Financial Impact of February 2021 Winter Storm.* State of Texas, 2021.

Zetter, Kim. *Countdown to Zero Day: Stuxnet and the Launch of the World's First Digital Weapon.* Crown, 2014.

**Healthcare Security & Regulation**

American Medical Informatics Association. "Framework for AI/ML-Based Clinical Decision Support." *Journal of the American Medical Informatics Association*, 2023.

Bates, David W., and Suchi Saria, et al. "A Systematic Review of the Application of Machine Learning in Health Care." *NPJ Digital Medicine*, 2019.

CommonSpirit Health. *Notice of Data Security Incident.* CommonSpirit Health, 2022.

Food and Drug Administration. *Artificial Intelligence/Machine Learning (AI/ML)-Based Software as a Medical Device (SaMD) Action Plan.* U.S. FDA, 2021.

Obermeyer, Ziad, et al. "Dissecting Racial Bias in an Algorithm Used to Manage the Health of Populations." *Science* 366, no. 6464 (2019): 447-453.

Office for Civil Rights. *HIPAA Security Rule Guidance on Risk Analysis.* U.S. Department of Health and Human Services, 2023.

Office of the National Coordinator for Health Information Technology. *21st Century Cures Act: Interoperability, Information Blocking, and the ONC Health IT Certification Program Final Rule.* U.S. Department of Health and Human Services, 2020.

Scripps Health. *Notice of Data Security Incident.* Scripps Health, 2021.

Universal Health Services. *Form 10-K Annual Report.* U.S. Securities and Exchange Commission, 2021.

**Financial Services Security & Regulation**

Bank for International Settlements. *Principles for the Sound Management of Operational Risk.* Basel Committee on Banking Supervision, 2021.

Board of Governors of the Federal Reserve System and Office of the Comptroller of the Currency. *Supervisory Guidance on Model Risk Management (SR 11-7).* Federal Reserve, 2011.

Commodity Futures Trading Commission and Securities and Exchange Commission. *Findings Regarding the Market Events of May 6, 2010.* CFTC/SEC, 2010.

European Parliament and Council. *Regulation (EU) 2024/1689: Artificial Intelligence Act.* Official Journal of the European Union, 2024.

Financial Stability Board. *Artificial Intelligence and Machine Learning in Financial Services.* FSB, 2017.

Kirilenko, Andrei A., et al. "The Flash Crash: High-Frequency Trading in an Electronic Market." *Journal of Finance* 72, no. 3 (2017): 967-998.

**Cross-Sector AI Security**

Anthropic. *Core Views on AI Safety.* Anthropic, 2023.

Carlini, Nicholas, et al. "Extracting Training Data from Large Language Models." *30th USENIX Security Symposium*, 2021.

Cybersecurity and Infrastructure Security Agency *Cross-Sector Cybersecurity Performance Goals.* Cybersecurity and Infrastructure Security Agency, 2023.

Cybersecurity and Infrastructure Security Agency *Emergency Directive 21-01: Mitigate SolarWinds Orion Code Compromise.* CISA, 2020 (updated 2021).

Goodfellow, Ian J., Jonathon Shlens, and Christian Szegedy. "Explaining and Harnessing Adversarial Examples." *International Conference on Learning Representations*, 2015.

Greshake Tzovaras, Kai, et al. "Not What You've Signed Up For: Compromising Real-World LLM-Integrated Applications with Indirect Prompt Injection." *arXiv preprint*, 2023.

MITRE. *ATLAS (Adversarial Threat Landscape for AI Systems)*. MITRE Corporation, 2023.

National Institute of Standards and Technology. *AI Risk Management Framework (AI RMF 1.0)*. NIST, 2023.

Perez, Ethan, et al. "Ignore This Title and HackAPrompt: Exposing Systemic Vulnerabilities of LLMs through a Global Scale Prompt Hacking Competition." *arXiv preprint*, 2023.

**Systemic Risk & Interdependencies**

Haldane, Andrew G., and Robert M. May. "Systemic Risk in Banking Ecosystems." *Nature* 469 (2011): 351-355.

Hollnagel, Erik. *Safety-I and Safety-II: The Past and Future of Safety Management*. Ashgate, 2014.

Perrow, Charles. *Normal Accidents: Living with High-Risk Technologies*. Princeton University Press, 1984.

Taleb, Nassim Nicholas. *Antifragile: Things That Gain from Disorder*. Random House, 2012.

Woods, David D., and John Wreathall. "Stress-Strain Plots as a Basis for Assessing System Resilience." *Resilience*

*Engineering: Concepts and Precepts*, edited by Erik Hollnagel et al., Ashgate, 2006.

**Human Factors & Workforce**

Bainbridge, Lisanne. "Ironies of Automation." *Automatica* 19, no. 6 (1983): 775-779.

Gates, Dominic. "Boeing's 737 MAX: A Failure of Management, Not Just Engineering." *Seattle Times*, 2019.

House Committee on Transportation and Infrastructure. *Final Committee Report: The Design, Development & Certification of the Boeing 737 MAX*. U.S. House of Representatives, 2020.

Parasuraman, Raja, and Victor Riley. "Humans and Automation: Use, Misuse, Disuse, Abuse." *Human Factors* 39, no. 2 (1997): 230-253.

**Sector-Specific Standards & Guidance**

American Water Works Association. *Cybersecurity Guidance for the Water Sector*. AWWA, 2023.

Cybersecurity and Infrastructure Security Agency Industrial Control Systems Cyber Emergency Response Team (ICS-CERT). *Advisories and Reports*. CISA, 2015-2024.

Health Information Sharing and Analysis Center (H-ISAC). *Threat Intelligence Reports*. H-ISAC, 2023-2024.

Transportation Security Administration. *Security Directive Pipeline-2021-02*. TSA, 2021.

**Complementary Resources**

Electricity Information Sharing and Analysis Center (E-ISAC). https://www.eisac.com/. Sector-specific threat intelligence and information sharing for electric utilities.

Financial Services Information Sharing and Analysis Center (FS-ISAC). https://www.fsisac.com/. Threat intelligence and coordination for financial services cybersecurity.

Health Information Sharing and Analysis Center (H-ISAC). https://h-isac.org/. Healthcare-specific cybersecurity intelligence and collaboration.

Partnership for AI. https://partnershiponai.org/. Multi-stakeholder organization addressing AI's impact across sectors.

Water Information Sharing and Analysis Center (WaterISAC). https://www.waterisac.org/. Security resources and threat intelligence for water and wastewater utilities.

www.ingramcontent.com/pod-product-compliance
Lightning Source LLC
La Vergne TN
LVHW050814061126
851857LV00012B/804